THE BEST HIKES OF PISGAH NATIONAL FOREST

JOHN F. BLAIR, PUBLISHER
WINSTON-SALEM, NORTH CAROLINA

THE
BEST
HIKES OF

Pisgah National Forest

BY

C. FRANKLIN GOLDSMITH, III
SHANNON E. G. HAMRICK
H. JAMES HAMRICK, JR.

Published by John F. Blair, Publisher

Fifth Printing

*The paper in this book meets the guidelines for
permanence and durability of the Committee
on Production Guidelines for Book Longevity
of the Council on Library Resources.*

Library of Congress Cataloging-in-Publication Data

Goldsmith, C. Franklin, 1974-
   The best hikes of Pisgah National Forest / by C. Franklin Goldsmith, III, Shannon E.G.
Hamrick, H. James Hamrick, Jr.
      p.   cm.
   Includes index.
   ISBN 13: 978-0-89587-190-9 (alk. paper)
   ISBN 10: 0-89587-190-4 (alk. paper)
   1. Hiking—North Carolina—Pisgah National Forest—Guidebooks. 2. Pisgah National
Forest (N.C.)—Guidebooks. I. Title: Pisgah National Forest. II. Hamrick, Shannon E.G.
III. Hamrick, H. James, 1970- IV. Title.

GV199.42.N66 G64 2000
917.56'93—dc21

                                                                                    00-056411

*All photos by authors unless otherwise noted
Design by Debra Long Hampton
Cover photograph copyright © Bill Lea
Composition by The Roberts Group*

DEDICATION

In memory of
C. Frank "Goldy" Goldsmith, Sr.,
who taught his grandchildren
to love and cherish
the North Carolina mountains

CONTENTS

PISGAH RANGER DISTRICT

Black Balsam Knob and Shining Rock Wilderness Area

Davidson River Valley

Avery Creek Area

Courthouse Creek Area

Other Trails in the Pisgah Ranger District

GRANDFATHER RANGER DISTRICT

Linville Gorge Wilderness Area

Harper Creek Area

Max Patch Area

Other Trails in the French Broad Ranger District

APPENDIX

PREFACE

The land comprising Pisgah National Forest has been a source of recreation and beauty for hikers of many generations. As long as people have enjoyed the simple pleasure of a walk in the woods, Pisgah has been a favorite place to shun civilization and immerse oneself in nature. The beauty of the trees, rivers, and trails is timeless. To sit or stroll quietly in a remote region of Pisgah is to experience the world as our ancestors did.

This book owes its existence in large part to one of our ancestors, C. Frank "Goldy" Goldsmith of Marion, North Carolina. He taught his grandchildren to explore and to appreciate Pisgah National Forest. Though he was no professional outdoorsman, he loved and respected this land. Many of the trails in this guide were his favorites and have become ours, too.

The hikes we have selected represent the best of what Pisgah National Forest has to offer in terms of three broad categories: views, waterfalls, and diversity of plant and animal life. Our choices are based on years of personal experience hiking in Pisgah, and we feel confident that novices, day hikers, and experienced trekkers alike will enjoy the guide as a tool for their own exploration of the national forest. We recognize the absurdity in claiming to have detailed the "best" hikes in Pisgah; hiking is not and never will be a competitive endeavor, and beauty and enjoyment are no more quantifiable than love. Still, the trails herein lead to some beautiful places, and it is sometimes hard to avoid superlatives in describing them.

We wrote this book with increased enjoyment of the overall hiking experience as a goal. To that end, we have organized the guide to minimize some of the difficulties we have encountered as hikers over the years. Inaccurate directions, poor estimations of distances, and poor trail descriptions can turn a pleasant day of hiking into a hurried, stressful, unrelaxing experience. Our guide is designed to avoid these pitfalls. Users will be able to find the trailheads quickly and not be uncertain when they come to forks in the trails. They also will be able to make it home in time for dinner, unless they choose to dally on some mountaintop.

The trails are organized geographically. Maps included in the book are based on United States Geological Survey (USGS) maps. Pisgah National Forest is divided into four ranger districts: Pisgah, Grandfather, Toecane, and French Broad. We have separated the trails according to the ranger districts. We have also included a number of sidebars on historical, natural, and medical topics related to Pisgah National Forest.

The hikes are formatted to make the selection process easy and quick. At the beginning of each hike, the reader will find the trail's length, its difficulty rating, its elevation change, its USGS map quadrant, and detailed directions to the trailhead.

The number following each trail name—for example, Cold Mountain Trail (#39)—is the standard number given to that trail by the Forest Service. Therefore, these trail numbers are consistent with the numbers used in other books and on other maps. Each hike is plotted on a topographical map; frequently, compass bearings to visible peaks are included. Each hike is described in detail. Prominent features, forks in the trail, distances covered, and expected flora are all remarked upon. The descriptions will enable hikers to choose a trail based on things they want to encounter, such as vistas, waterfalls, and plant life. And during the hike, the descriptions and sidebars will enhance participants' appreciation of the surroundings.

A special feature of this hiking guide is the inclusion of global positioning system (GPS) coordinates. For the technologically inclined hiker, a hand-held GPS can be a helpful and fun tool to carry on the trail, providing information on location, distance traveled, interesting way points, and elevation. No other guide to Pisgah National Forest includes GPS coordinates, and few hiking guides anywhere have taken advantage of this technology. Now that GPS systems are compact and affordable, we expect the inclusion of coordinates in hiking guides to become commonplace.

Ultimately, we hope that this guide will enable and encourage people to explore Pisgah National Forest and discover it for themselves. Walking in the woods is one of life's simplest pleasures. You really don't need much more than the clothes on your back, a keen sensorium, and some sense of where you're going. Frank "Goldy" Goldsmith helped show us where to go, and we hope to do the same for readers of this guide.

ACKNOWLEDGMENTS

The authors would like to thank Laura Dover Doran, for her encouragement, ideas, and indexing; Carolyn Sakowski, for her wisdom and patience; our parents—Dianne Tuttle, for always making us stop to notice the wildflowers, Frank Goldsmith, for making us hiking enthusiasts at a young age, and Harvey and Ann Hamrick, for their love; Diamond Brand Outdoor Equipment of Naples, North Carolina, for supplies and support, with special thanks to Gary Eblin; Mary Hiers and Dave Danly, for their botanical knowledge and hiking companionship; and Wilma Dykeman, for her generosity and example.

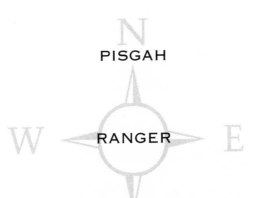

PISGAH

W   RANGER   E

DISTRICT

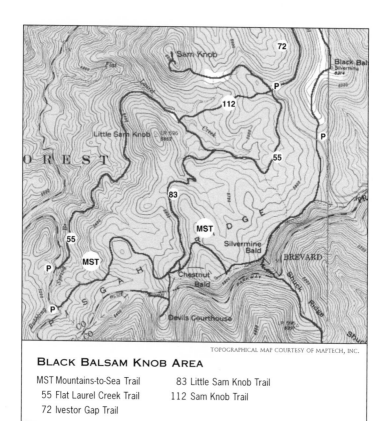

TOPOGRAPHICAL MAP COURTESY OF MAPTECH, INC.

BLACK BALSAM KNOB AREA

MST Mountains-to-Sea Trail   83 Little Sam Knob Trail
  55 Flat Laurel Creek Trail   112 Sam Knob Trail
  72 Ivestor Gap Trail

BLACK BALSAM KNOB AND SHINING ROCK WILDERNESS AREA

The Shining Rock Wilderness Area, created in 1964, was originally composed of 13,600 acres. In 1984, the North Carolina Wilderness Act increased the area to its current 18,500 acres. Shining Rock derives its name from its unusually large quartz outcropping, which has always been shrouded in mystery and legend among both the native Cherokees and European settlers.

Boasting nearly 3,000 feet in elevation change, the Shining Rock Wilderness Area is strikingly diverse. It has low-elevation acidic coves, mile-high bogs, Canadian spruce/fir forests, high-elevation heath balds and grassy knobs, rich cove forests, and Northern hardwood forests. The area is centered around the nearly 6,000-foot-high Shining Rock Ridge. Cold Mountain, at 6,030 feet, is the highest peak in the ridge. On either side of the ridge begin the headwaters of the Pigeon River; both the East Fork and the West Fork offer incredible opportunities to swim, fish, and just rock-hop.

As a wilderness area, Shining Rock enjoys certain protections to help preserve the pristine environment. The trails are not groomed or maintained like other parts of the national forest, nor are there frequent blazes or signs indicating trail junctions. Thus, good back-country skills and preparation are a must.

Of the trails described below, only eight—Art Loeb IV, Cold Mountain, Shining Creek, Old Butt Knob, Big East Fork, Greasy Cove, and portions of Art Loeb III and Ivestor Gap—are technically within the boundaries of the wilderness area. Perhaps one day, those boundaries will be extended southward toward the parkway. Until then, the remaining trails do not share similar protection. However, because these trails are so closely linked physically, we have included all of them in this chapter.

The most commonly used access to these magnificent trails is from the Black Balsam Parking Area. At Milepost 420.2 on the Blue Ridge Parkway, turn north on to S.R. 816, following the signs for Black Balsam Trail Area. The road crosses the Mountains-to-Sea Trail and the Art Loeb Trail after 0.8 mile, where there is lots of parking on both sides, and terminates at a large parking lot at 1.2 miles. There are four official trailheads here: Flat Laurel Creek Trail and Sam Knob Trail are at the southern end of the lot, Sam Knob Summit Trail is behind the restroom facility to the west, and the Ivestor Gap Trail begins at the gated road to the northeast (35° 19' 31", W 82° 52' 55").

SAM KNOB SUMMIT TRAIL

Length: 1.2 miles one way
Difficulty: moderate to strenuous
Elevation change: 400 feet
USGS quadrant: Sam Knob
Access: Take the Blue Ridge Parkway to the Black Balsam
  Knob Parking Area at Milepost 420.2. There is an
  outhouse at the end of the parking lot; to the west
  behind the outhouse is a gated roadbed. The trail
  begins behind gate (N 25° 19' 32", W 82° 52' 55").
  See map on page 2.

This is a new trail in the Black Balsam Knob area and isn't printed on most maps.

The trail begins behind the gate and follows a flat, old roadbed through fire cherry, bush honeysuckle, viburnum, hypericum, gooseberry, and blackberry. You will reach a large, grassy clearing after 0.4 mile; this clearing is the site of extensive research by the forest department, so please do not venture off the trail or disturb the soil. At the end of the meadow, the trail looks like it could go in any of three directions; however, the trails to the left and directly in front are abandoned. The Sam Knob Summit Trail begins 30 yards to the right, marked by a carsonite sign. The narrow ascent follows a series of moderate switchbacks through a heath bald as the trail wraps around the southern side of Sam Knob. After 1 mile, the trail comes to a T intersection; to the right, it ascends toward the southern summit, and to the left, it ascends toward the northern summit. From the southern summit, you can enjoy outstanding views of Tennent Mountain at 69° and 1.5 miles, Black Balsam Knob at 94° and 1.1 miles, Fork River Bald at 121° and

2.1 miles, Devil's Courthouse at 187° and 1.7 miles, Bruce Knob at 196° and 5.7 miles, Little Sam Knob at 201° and 0.5 mile, Tanasee Bald at 212° and 2.8 miles, Mount Hardy at 233° and 2.5 miles, Gage Bald at 256° and 4.8 miles, Rough Butt Bald at 262° and 4.1 miles, and Reinhart Knob at 292° and 4.9 miles. From the northern summit, you can see Balsam Knob at 300° and 6 miles, Cold Spring Knob at 318° and 6.1 miles, Lickstone Bald at 331° and 7.9 miles, Birdstand Mountain at 353° and 2.3 miles, High Top at 347° and 4 miles, Ratcliff Mountain at 355° and 11 miles, Max Patch at 358° and 32.5 miles, Chambers Mountain at 2° and 16.5 miles, Camp Creek Bald at 16° and 49 miles, Cold Mountain at 25° and 5.9 miles, Shining Rock at 40° and 3.2 miles, and Mount Mitchell at 54° and 46.5 miles.

SAM KNOB TRAIL (#112)

Length: 0.9 mile one way
Difficulty: easy
Elevation change: 400 feet
USGS quadrant: Sam Knob
Access: At Milepost 420.2 on the Blue Ridge Parkway, turn north on to the road marked "Black Balsam Trail Area." See map on page 2.

From the parking lot, the trail descends along a narrow, eroded path through grass, viburnum, blueberry, bluets, dwarf cinquefoil, cinnamon fern, and sphagnum moss. You will enjoy beautiful views of Sam Knob, Little Sam Knob, and the mile-high grassy, boggy, rolling fields that are the headwaters for Flat Laurel Creek. There is a large campsite to the right at 0.8 mile, and numerous other camping possibilities are located nearby (N 19' 25", W 53' 37"). Fifty yards later, the trail passes beneath a large red spruce in a dense thicket and crosses Flat Laurel Creek. It ends on the other side of the creek at the intersection with the Flat Laurel Creek Trail (N 19' 22", W 53' 38").

LITTLE SAM KNOB TRAIL (#83)

Length: 1.4 miles one way
Difficulty: easy
Elevation change: 250 feet
USGS quadrant: Sam Knob
Access: There are two trailheads for the Little Sam Knob
Trail. The northern trailhead is off the Flat Laurel
Creek Trail 1.1 mile from the Black Balsam Parking
Area (N 19' 10", W 53' 22"). The southern trailhead is
off the Mountains-to-Sea Trail just northwest of
Chestnut Bald (N 18' 25", W 53' 41"). See map on
page 2.

From the carsonite sign on the Flat Laurel Creek Trail, you will turn on to a narrow, rocky path lined with blackberry, red spruce, and rhododendron. After 0.5 mile, the trail crosses a small creek. You will make a sharp right turn at a carsonite sign up the hill from the creek (N 18' 57", W 53' 33"). Just beyond this potentially confusing intersection are nice views through mountain ash of Little Sam Knob (336° and 0.4 mile) and Sam Knob (0° and 0.9 mile). A quarter-mile later, the trail bends to the left and heads south, where you will enjoy excellent views over the West Fork of the Pigeon River into Middle Prong Wilderness Area; the highest knob in the distance is Mount Hardy, 2 miles west-southwest. The trail crosses a small gulch at 1.3 mile (N 18' 55", W 53' 42"). The narrow path to the left up the gulch is the old route for the Little Sam Knob Trail; the trails reconnect after 0.2 mile. There is a nice campsite in a field of grass and sedge at 1.4 mile (N 18' 27", W 53' 41"). Thirty yards beyond the campsite, the Little Sam Knob Trail ends at the intersection with the Mountains-to-Sea Trail. If you go left on the Mountains-to-Sea Trail I, the old Little Sam Knob Trail enters from the left after 0.1 mile; it is marked by a carsonite sign (N 18' 26", W 53' 36"). If you go right on the Mountains-to-Sea Trail II, it is 0.4 mile to the parking lot at Devil's Courthouse on the Blue Ridge Parkway and 1.8 miles to N.C. 215.

MOUNTAINS-TO-SEA TRAIL I
Length: 2.2 miles one way
Difficulty: easy
Elevation change: 280 feet
USGS quadrant: Sam Knob
Access: There are two intersections that define the ends of this section of the MST. The western trailhead begins at the end of the Little Sam Knob Trail (N 18' 25", W 53' 41"). The eastern trailhead is on Black Balsam Parking Area Road 0.8 mile north of the Blue Ridge Parkway (N 19' 13", W 52' 34"). See map on page 2.

Begin at the junction with the Little Sam Knob Trail, where you will turn left (northeast). After 0.1 mile, you will pass the old terminus of the Little Sam Knob Trail, marked by a carsonite sign. After another 0.1 mile, you will see a rock outcropping to the left; from the top, there are excellent views of Sam Knob, Little Sam Knob, and Mount Hardy. The trail follows an easy-to-moderate ascent for the next 0.3 mile through a heath bald. A sign on a tree at 0.8 mile indicates that you are now entering the jurisdiction of the National Park Service. Twenty yards later, a spur trail breaks off to the right and passes through a dense thicket of Pierus to a rock outcropping on the southeastern side of Chestnut Bald (N 18' 24", W 53' 14"). The rock affords an incredible vista of the Davidson River Valley to the southeast and the headwaters of the French Broad River to the south. The sharp peak directly across is Pilot Mountain (158° and 2.6 miles). Looking across the Davidson River Valley, you see Black Mountain at 85° and 8.7 miles, Looking Glass Rock at 97° and 5.3 miles, John Rock at 113° and 5.8 miles, and Cedar Rock at 130° and 5.9 miles. To the southwest are Toxaway Mountain at 208° and 13.2 miles and Bald Knob at 211° and 4.7 miles on the long Tanasee Ridge, which divides Pisgah National Forest from Nantahala National Forest, Transylvania County from Jackson County, and the French Broad River Valley from the Tuckasegee River Valley. A tenth of a mile past the overlook, the trail descends to an open, grassy meadow with a small campsite (N 18' 27", W 53' 10"). From the saddle, you will begin a short, moderate ascent up Silvermine Bald through lots of pinkshell azalea (which is native only to North Carolina), yellow bead lily, Canadian mayflower, and trillium. The Art Loeb Trail intersects the Mountains-to-Sea Trail at 1 mile (N 18' 31", W 53' 0"). To the right, the Art Loeb Trail/Mountains-to-Sea Trail Alternate descends 0.2 mile to the Blue Ridge Parkway. You will reach a small campsite with a nice view of Pilot Mountain and Cedar Rock at 1.5 mile; beyond the campsite, the trail passes through a large stand of red spruce. In another 0.5 mile, you will reach a campsite on an exposed, grassy hilltop (N 19' 6", W 52' 33"). The trail passes beneath another spruce grove before reaching a road 0.1 mile later (N 19' 13", W 52' 34"). Across the road, the Art Loeb Trail ascends Black Balsam Knob and the Mountains-to-Sea Trail descends to Graveyard Ridge. To the left, it is 0.4 mile to the Black Balsam Parking Area.

FLAT LAUREL CREEK TRAIL (#55)

Length: 3.7 miles one way
Difficulty: easy
Elevation change: 800 feet
USGS quadrant: Sam Knob
Access: This trail has two trailheads. To reach the
    northeastern trailhead, take the Blue Ridge Parkway to
    the Black Balsam Parking Area (35° 19' 31", W 82°
    52' 55"). For the southwestern trailhead, take the Blue
    Ridge Parkway to N.C. 215 North, drive 0.9 mile,
    and turn right into the small parking area (N 18' 27",
    W 54' 32"). See map on page 2.

At the trailhead off N.C. 215, you will begin on a dirt road and cross Bubbling Spring Branch after 50 yards. Twenty yards past the crossing, you will reach a large campsite to the left. The wide roadbed is lined with rhododendron, viburnum, black birch, mountain laurel, and Fraser fir. There is a small waterfall to the right at 0.2 mile, and a second, much larger waterfall at a cement bridge at 0.7 mile. After 1 mile, the trail crosses a branch and faces Sam Knob to the north-northwest. You'll reach a good campsite on the left at 1.2 mile, beneath a black and a yellow birch; there are nice views to the northwest here. Through the opening at 1.5 miles, you'll enjoy excellent views of Fork Ridge. A small spur trail descends to the left at 1.8 miles. This is a genuine siren's song of a trail; the deceptive sounds of falling water may lure you down this steep trail in hopes that it might lead to a perfect vantage point or a hidden swimming hole. It doesn't; instead, the trail runs straight down the mountainside to N.C. 215, the creek is *never* visible, and the hike back up is positively hellish. A tenth of a mile later, you'll reach a washed-out area in the trail. To the left is a very steep, dangerous descent to a good pool in the waterfall; there is a marginally "safer" scramble down to the falls 50 yards later, but it, too, is quite dangerous. Only someone with the confidence of a mountain goat should attempt this descent. Flat Laurel Creek Falls is an unbroken sequence of waterfalls that cascades for nearly 0.5 mile and offers numerous small swimming holes for those willing to seek them out. The small trail to the left at 2.2 miles goes to the top of the waterfall and a campsite; a second campsite is just past this intersection. An excellent, large campsite rests beneath a grove of red spruce at 2.3 miles. A tenth of a mile later, the creek valley opens up, and you'll find lots of willow, blackberry, blueberry, gooseberry, and St.-John's-wort; a small campsite is to the left. The Sam Knob Trail comes in from the left 50 yards later. Fifty yards beyond the trail junction is another good campsite. You will cross a small branch and pass a small campsite on the right at 2.5 miles (N 19' 16", W 53' 34"). A tenth of a mile later, the trail passes through a large, pure stand of yellow birch in a picture-perfect Northern hardwood forest. The Little Sam Knob Trail begins to the left at 2.7 miles (N 19' 10", W 53' 22"). The rocky roadbed continues through fire cherry, yellow and sweet birch, rhododendron, Pierus, mountain laurel, flame azalea, and saxifrage; to the left are nice views of Sam Knob and rolling, grassy fields. The trail crosses a spring near a young spruce grove at 3.3 miles. A tenth of a mile later, you will reach an excellent, small campsite to the left overlooking the meadow. From here, the trail follows the roadbed

GPS

Global Positioning System (GPS) is a navigational tool that is rapidly gaining acceptance among hikers. Given the increase in accuracy and the decrease in cost of light, portable units, it's easy to see why these machines can be useful in the wilderness.

A GPS unit works by receiving data from a system of satellites. The United States Department of Defense currently maintains 24 satellites in orbit that are available for civilian use. The satellites blanket the earth and provide positioning and timing information. A hand-held GPS unit receives data from these satellites and processes the information. By simple triangulation, it can pinpoint the location of the user with startling accuracy.

In principle, the satellites can locate an object within an inch. However, for reasons of national security, such precise data is not available to the public. Previously, the Department of Defense instituted a policy known as Selective Availability. Under this policy, satellite signals were downgraded or scrambled, so that the accuracy of civilian units suffered. GPS units were typically accurate to within 30 meters but could often be off by as much as 100 meters.

As of May 1, 2000, however, the Department of Defense discontinued its policy of Selective Availability. Now, the same hand-held GPS units are accurate to within 20 meters. Unfortunately, this book was written prior to May 1, 2000, so all of the GPS data in it was collected during the period of Selective Availability. To ensure minimal error, the authors took the GPS data for particular locations several different times over extended intervals on different days, then averaged the data to improve accuracy.

In this book, GPS data is in parentheses following specific

locations—a trail junction, a mountain summit, a campsite, or other point of interest. The data is given in the usual form—degrees, minutes, and seconds of latitude and longitude. For example, the location of the trailhead for the Sam Knob Trail is given as (N 25° 19' 32", W 82° 52' 55"). Typically, we give the trailhead location in degrees, minutes, and seconds; after that, we give only the minutes and seconds. This is because a degree of latitude or longitude is so large (more than 100 kilometers) that it will not change in the course of one hike. Thus, continuing our example, the next point on the Sam Knob Trail is given as (N 19' 25", W 53' 37").

Thanks to improved accuracy, a typical hand-held unit will be accurate to within one second of latitude or longitude. It is possible, however, that your GPS unit and the data in the book will disagree by as much as three seconds.

Therefore, if you are looking for a particular point—say, a hard-to-find trail junction—and your GPS differs from the data in the book by four seconds or more, then you're not at that particular junction.

Despite the obvious navigational benefits, a GPS unit is not an idiot-proof way to avoid getting lost in the woods. These devices take some getting used to and should not be relied upon too heavily. Natural obstructions like steep valley walls and mountain peaks will block satellite signals and greatly decrease the accuracy of small, hand-held units. For example, it is extremely difficult to get a reliable reading when you are in the deepest coves of Linville Gorge. Therefore, while they are undeniably handy devices, GPS units are no substitute for good, old-fashioned back-country skills like being able to use a topo map and a compass.

for 0.25 mile as it bends to the left. A tenth of a mile later, the trail ends at the Black Balsam Parking Area after 3.7 miles (35° 19' 31", W 82° 52' 55").

MOUNTAINS-TO-SEA TRAIL II

Length: 2.1 miles one way
Difficulty: easy to moderate
Elevation change: 680 feet
USGS quadrant: Sam Knob
Access: There are two trailheads for this section of the
     Mountains-to-Sea Trail. The western trailhead, on N.C.
     215, is 0.6 mile north of the Blue Ridge Parkway
     (N 18' 13", W 54' 33"). The eastern trailhead is at the
     end of the Little Sam Knob Trail (N 18' 25",
     W 53' 41"). See map on page 2.

From the junction with the Little Sam Knob Trail, turn to the right (west) and begin an easy descent through red spruce, yellow birch, mountain ash, high-bush blueberry, and rhododendron. After 100 yards, the trail crosses a large rock with a dot and an arrow painted on it, then bends to the left; directly to the south is Devil's Courthouse. There is a trail junction 100 yards later; the trail to the left goes 0.25 mile to the summit of Devil's Courthouse, and the 0.5-mile detour is *well* worth it. Just after passing an exceptionally tall grove of rhododendron at 0.3 mile, you will enjoy nice views of Mount Hardy at 266° and 1.7 miles and Rough Butt Bald at 281° and 3.8 miles. The trail continues to the right of a massive grove of pure red spruce and to the left of a grassy meadow filled with hay-scented fern, yellow birch, and rhododendron. After 0.5 mile, it enters the spruce grove; the deep, perpetually blanketed floor of spruce needles masks the trail completely, so you must follow the white dots on the trees to find your way out. Two tenths of a mile later, the trail leaves the spruce grove and enters a Northern hardwood forest. It bends sharply to the right at 1.2 miles and begins a moderate descent into a mixed hardwood forest. You will come to a stream with two logs crossing it at 1.6 miles. You should not cross here; turn to the right and cross the stream 50 yards later. The trail ends at 2.1 miles on N.C. 215 (N 18' 13", W 54' 33"). There are a couple of trail signs here, and a small gravel pullout is across the road beside a couple of trail signs. To the left, it is 0.6 mile south to the Blue Ridge Parkway. To the right, it is 0.3 mile north to the parking area for the Flat Laurel Creek Trail.

IVESTOR GAP TRAIL (#72)

Length: 4.3 miles one way
Difficulty: easy
Elevation change: 200 feet
USGS quadrants: Sam Knob, Shining Rock
Access: This trail is accessed from the Black Balsam
    Parking Area. It begins behind the gated dirt road to
    the north (35° 19' 31", W 82° 52' 55"). See map on
    page 2.

The Ivestor Gap Trail follows an old dirt road north from the Black Balsam Parking Area to Ivestor Gap. The hike offers several spectacular views to the west and north of the West Fork of the Pigeon River and the Great Balsam Mountains. The trail winds its way north, enters the Shining Rock Wilderness Area at Wash Hollow, crosses Fork Mountain Ridge, and reaches a small saddle after 1.8 miles; the Art Loeb Trail, marked by a wooden sign, descends from the right to join the Ivestor Gap Trail. The two trails run conjunctively for the next 50 yards, then the Art Loeb Trail forks off to the right and enters a pine grove. The Ivestor Gap Trail continues on the roadbed to the left of the knob for 0.5 mile before reaching several trail junctions in Ivestor Gap at 2.3 miles (N 20' 43", W 52' 2"). To the left behind the wooden sign, the Ivestor Gap Trail continues northbound on an old roadbed; ahead and to the left, the Art Loeb Trail follows a narrow foot trail that ascends to the right of Grassy Cove Top; the dirt road straight ahead is the Graveyard Ridge Trail; and to the right, the Art Loeb Trail descends from a small pine grove. After 3.5 miles, the Ivestor Gap Trail crosses a small spring; shortly thereafter, the faint Little East Fork Trail forks off to the left. A tenth of a mile later, the trail bends to the left, wraps around a ridge for 0.25 mile, then turns sharply to the right, where it offers outstanding views to the northwest of High Top and the basin of the West Fork of the Pigeon River. You will arrive in Shining Rock Gap after 4.3 miles (N 21' 51", W 51' 49"). There are multiple trail junctions here. Immediately to the left, the Art Loeb Trail continues on the old roadbed towards Stairs Mountain; ahead and to the left, the Old Butt Knob Trail ascends toward Shining Rock; and ahead and to the right, the Art Loeb Trail continues toward Flower Knob.

Length: 7 miles one way
Difficulty: moderate for the first 4 miles, strenuous
    thereafter
Elevation change: 1,100 feet
USGS quadrants: Sam Knob, Shining Rock, Cruso
Access: This section of the Art Loeb Trail begins on F.R.
    816 at the Black Balsam Parking Area, 0.8 mile north
    of the Blue Ridge Parkway. The trailhead is on the
    right. There is ample parking on both sides of the
    road (N 35° 19' 14", W 82° 52' 34"). See maps on
    pages 18–19.

The Mountains-to-Sea Trail and the Art Loeb Trail begin at the same point, but after 10 yards, the Mountains-to-Sea Trail descends to the right and the Art Loeb Trail continues straight ahead up Black Balsam Knob. It is a moderate ascent up the grassy bald through lots of blueberry. You will reach the top of a knob after 0.3 mile, then descend into a small saddle before beginning a moderate-to-strenuous ascent. The trail crests Black Balsam Knob at 0.6 mile (N 19' 39", W 52' 28"), where a small plaque commemorates the Art Loeb Trail. You will enjoy an outstanding panorama from the summit. Beginning to the north, you will see Cold Mountain at 14° and 5.8 miles, Camp Creek Bald at 15° and 48.9 miles, Shining Rock at 18° and 2.7 miles, Rocky Face Mountain at 28° and 10.4 miles, Old Butt Knob at 34° and 3.5 miles, Mount Pisgah at 48° and 9.5 miles, Fryingpan Mountain at 55° and 7.2 miles, Mount Mitchell at 55° and 45.7 miles, Green Knob at 69° and 4.6 miles, Black Mountain at 94° and 7.9 miles, Looking Glass Rock at 114° and 4.7 miles, John Rock at 129° and 5.8 miles, Cedar Rock at 144° and 6.4 miles, Pilot Mountain 178° and 3.8 miles, Mount Hardy at 245° and

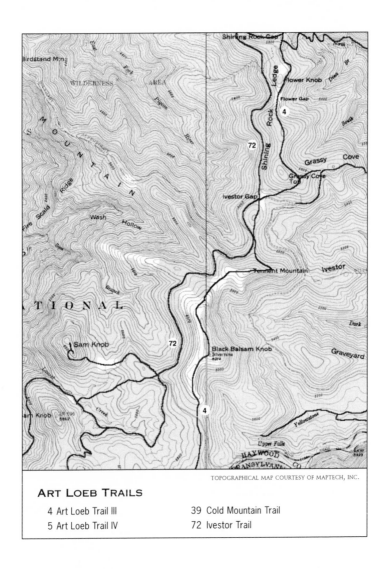

TOPOGRAPHICAL MAP COURTESY OF MAPTECH, INC.

Art Loeb Trails

4 Art Loeb Trail III
5 Art Loeb Trail IV

39 Cold Mountain Trail
72 Ivestor Trail

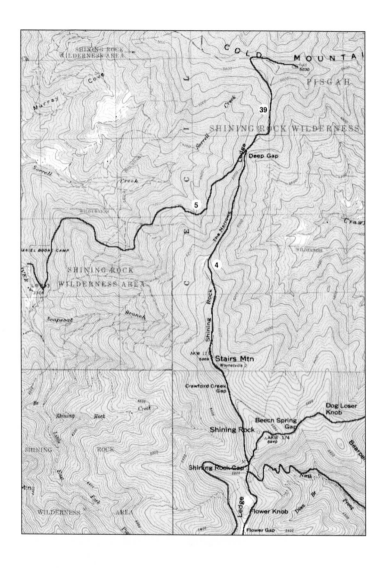

3.4 miles, Balsam Knob at 297° and 7.1 miles, Clingmans Dome at 299° and 38.7 miles, Grassy Bald at 307° and 12 miles, Cold Spring Knob at 312° and 7.1 miles, Lickstone Bald at 325° and 8.7 miles, Birdstand Mountain at 330° and 2.8 miles, High Top at 333° and 4.6 miles, and Max Patch at 356° and 32.8 miles. A spur trail breaks off to the left, but the main trail continues straight ahead, then begins a series of switchbacks before descending to a small saddle. It reaches the summit of Tennent Mountain at 1.6 miles (N 20' 13", W 52' 9"), where there is a marker in honor of Dr. Tennent. From the summit, you will continue east along Ivestor Ridge for 0.25 mile, make a sharp left, and descend to a junction with the Ivestor Gap Trail at 2.2 miles. The two trails run conjunctively for 50 yards, then the Art Loeb Trail forks off to the right. Shortly thereafter, you will come to a small but great campsite beneath a grove of pitch pine to the left. The trail crests a small knob, then descends through another pine grove to Ivestor Gap after 2.4 miles (N 20' 43", W 52' 3"). There is a large Forest Service sign in Ivestor Gap indicating that you are now entering Shining Rock Wilderness Area; there are also multiple trail junctions. The Ivestor Gap Trail bends around from the left on a gravel road, then continues straight ahead on a different old roadbed; the gravel road becomes the Graveyard Ridge Trail as it bends around to the right. The Art Loeb Trail turns right on the dirt road, follows it for 15 yards, then forks off to the left at a carsonite sign. It begins a moderate ascent of Grassy Cove Top through blueberry, blackberry, goldenrod, and occasional fire cherry before veering off to the right into a laurel slick as it wraps around the eastern side of the knob. Four tenths of a mile later, you will come to an easily missed trail junction where the Art Loeb/ Greasy Cove Connector Trail forks off to the right; there is a cherry tree stump to the right, a stand of maple to the left, and a downy serviceberry straight ahead (N 20' 49", W 51' 43").

At 3.1 miles, you will reach a wooden sign indicating that an old section of the trail has been closed and rerouted; ahead, the trail crests a small knob, then descends to Flower Gap at 3.6 miles, where there is a lovely grove of dwarf beech to the right. After 0.3 mile, you will pass a small spring to your right, marked by a faceless old sign nailed to a cherry tree; there is a second, larger spring 0.1 mile later, although the area surrounding it is closed for plant rehabilitation. Soon thereafter, the trail passes to the left of a magnificent spruce grove where the faint Shining Creek Trail drops down to the right. Fifty yards later, you will arrive at multiple trail junctions in Shining Rock Gap at 4.2 miles (N 21' 51", W 51' 49"). To the left immediately behind you, a spur trail goes to several campsites. Perpendicularly to the left, the Ivestor Gap Trail begins on an old roadbed. Straight ahead, there are three small trails: the trail to the right leads to a small campsite; the middle trail is the Old Butt Knob Trail; and the Art Loeb Trail continues ahead to the left on an old roadbed. (Note: If you want to see the quartz outcroppings of Shining Rock, you should take the Old Butt Knob Trail. After 100 yards, the trail becomes rather faint and veers to the right as you enter a rocky forest. Soon thereafter, a small spur trail forks off to the left and scrambles over some quartzite boulders to spectacular views to the south. A tenth of a mile later, a second spur trail forks off to the left and goes past an overused grassy campsite to the summit of Shining Rock.)

Leaving Shining Rock Gap, the Art Loeb Trail follows an old roadbed north on a flat, easy grade alongside a dense hedge of Pierus, red spruce, mountain laurel, and blueberry. Four tenths of a mile later, the trail narrows as it begins a moderate climb over rocky, root-cluttered terrain through beech, red oak, and red maple. You will crest Stairs Mountain at 5.1 miles; a spur trail to the right leads to a small rock overlook beneath a large red oak, where you can enjoy outstanding views to the northeast of Mount Pisgah at 66° and 7.2 miles and Cold Mountain at 21° and 2.4 miles. Descending Stairs Mountain, you will enter what is possibly the most sublime section of the whole trail as you pass along the spine of the mile-high ridge through Fraser fir, red spruce, Solomon's-seal, wild geranium, rosy twisted-stalk, thalictrum, cinnamon fern, galax, oak fern, white snake-root, and Turk's-cap lily. Nine tenths of a mile later, the trail begins a moderate-to-strenuous descent. You will pass a large, exposed rock to your left at 6.2 miles; from the top of the rock, you can enjoy spectacular views to the west of the West Prong of the Pigeon River and the Great Balsam Mountains; Birdstand Mountain is visible at 228° and 2.8 miles, Balsam Knob at 261° and 7 miles, High Top at 266° and 2.7 miles, Cold Spring Knob at 274° and 5.9 miles, Grassy Bald at 286° and 10.7 miles, Lickstone Bald at 297° and 6.3 miles, and Ratcliff Mountain at 338° and 7.4 miles. Beyond the rock, the trail begins a moderate descent to a small saddle, crests a small knob, then begins a strenuous descent to Deep Gap. Three quarters of a mile later, the descent ends as you emerge from a thick bramble of blackberry into a stand of pure locust. From here, you will ascend a small knob, pass a massive red oak surrounded by foamflower and jack-in-the-pulpit, and descend to Deep Gap. At 7 miles, the trail ends in Deep Gap, where you'll find a small clearing and a second locust grove. The Art Loeb Trail IV descends perpendicularly to the left; there is no sign to mark this junction, but the trailhead is easily distinguished. There are a few old sour apple trees here, remnants of the time when this ridge was cleared and used for grazing. A spring is located on the left 0.2 mile down the Art Loeb Trail. Straight ahead is the Cold Mountain Trail.

ART LOEB TRAIL IV

Length: 3.8 miles one way
Difficulty: strenuous
Elevation change: 1,800 feet
USGS quadrants: Cruso, Waynesville
Access: The eastern trailhead is in Deep Gap on Shining Rock Ledge (N 35° 24' 0", W 82° 51' 51"). The western trailhead is at Daniel Boone Boy Scout Camp (N 35° 23' 13", W 82° 53' 45"). See maps on pages 18–19.

It is impossible to do justice to the intense biodiversity of this trail; to list the flora encountered would be to catalog what must be the majority of plant species in this region. The reason that so many plants are represented is simple: the trail starts nearly a mile high and rapidly drops almost 2,000 feet through a series of dense coves, some of which face south, others north. You will begin at the lower tip of a spruce/fir forest, descend through an acidic cove forest, and end up in a rich hardwood forest, having passed dozens of wildflowers along the way. Perhaps the best times of the year to hike this trail are the transitional periods of spring and autumn, when the seasons differ at the top and bottom of the trail. Summer always comes sooner and stays longer at the base of the mountain. If you descend from Cold Mountain in the fall, for example, it feels as if you are walking back into summer; the leaves have fallen at the summit, but as you meander down the mountain, you will descend through all fall's glory and finish where the leaves are still green. It is possible—and highly recommended—to begin the Art Loeb Trail at Black Balsam Knob Parking Area, climb Cold Mountain, and descend to the Boy Scout Camp in one day. In doing so, you will avoid the brutal ascent of Cold Mountain and therefore might better appreciate the striking diversity the trail has to offer.

Beginning at the eastern trailhead in Deep Gap, the trail begins a moderate-to-strenuous descent through a forest with plentiful hemlock. You will cross a small spring on the left after 0.2 mile. For the next mile, the descent is moderate as the trail follows the contour of the ridge to the south-southwest. You will cross another spring after 1.3 miles, whereupon the trail enters a grove of massive hemlock trees. Leaving the hemlock grove, you will resume a moderate-to-strenuous descent. Three tenths of a mile later, you will cross a larger stream and enter a grove of yellow birch. Just prior to the 1.8-mile mark, the trail briefly follows an old roadbed, then forks off to the right. Less than 0.5 mile later, it briefly follows a second old logging road before forking to the right. From here, the trail slowly wraps around a large ridge jutting out to the northwest before descending steeply to the south. After 3.3 miles, the trail switches back several times, then heads north. The last 0.1 mile is brutally steep as you drop down to the dirt road at the Boy Scout camp.

COLD MOUNTAIN TRAIL (#39)

Length: 1.4 miles one way
Difficulty: strenuous
Elevation change: 1,000 feet
USGS quadrant: Cruso
Access: The trailhead is in Deep Gap on Shining Rock
   Ledge (N 35° 24' 0", W 82° 51' 51"). The shortest
   route to Deep Gap is to climb the Art Loeb Trail IV
   from Daniel Boone Boy Scout Camp. This ascent is
   very strenuous, however. The longer—though
   considerably less steep—route requires taking the Art
   Loeb Trail III north from the Black Balsam Knob
   Parking Area. Either way, the round trip will take a full
   day, and there is little reliable water along the way, so
   plan accordingly. See maps on pages 18–19.

From Deep Gap, the trail rapidly begins a strenuous climb through wood aster, white snakeroot, hawthorn, and other heath beneath a mixed hardwood canopy. Just prior to the 1-mile mark, you will find an unreliable, ephemeral spring; there is a small piece of PVC pipe coming out of the hillside to the right. The trail reaches the western ridge crest at 1.1 miles (N 24' 38", W 51' 49"), where you'll see a small campsite in a clearing, then bends sharply to the right as it begins the final ascent to the summit. One hundred yards later, there is an excellent campsite to the left in a grove of beech. After 1.5 miles, you will reach the summit of Cold Mountain, marked by a USGS survey marker stamped into a rock (N 24' 35", W 51' 25"). A small trail continues straight ahead to the east but eventually peters out as it descends off the mountain. For most of the 20th century, this summit was a grassy bald; however, since the area can no longer be cleared, the hardwoods are slowly recovering.

Thus, you will not find much in the way of views from the summit except in the winter months, when the foliage does not obstruct. Nonetheless, there is still one spectacular vista that more than justifies the strenuous ascent. From the summit, if you return 10 yards down the main trail, you will find a small spur trail that forks off to the left. If you follow this trail for several more yards, you will reach a large, exposed rock surface on the southern side of the summit. From here, you can enjoy one of the best panoramas anywhere in the region, encompassing the two forks of the Pigeon River, all of Shining Rock Wilderness Area, the Davidson River area, and the Great Balsam Mountains. Beginning in the east (to your left), you will see Mount Pisgah at 83° and 5.7 miles, Fryingpan Mountain at 108° and 4.8 miles, Beech Knob at 115° and 4.5 miles, Green Knob at 143° and 4.8 miles, Old Butt Knob at 167° and 2.7 miles, Shining Rock at 190° and 2.9 miles, Black Balsam Knob at 194° and 5.7 miles, Sam Knob at 205° and 6 miles, Mount Hardy at 213° and 8.3 miles, Birdstand Mountain at 222° and 4.2 miles, High Top at 246° and 3.8 miles, Balsam Knob at 253° and 8 miles, Cold Spring Knob at 263° and 6.7 miles, Laurel Patch Bald at 273° and 10.6 miles, and Lickstone Bald at 284° and 6.6 miles.

GREASY COVE TRAIL (#66)

Length: 3.2 miles one way
Difficulty: moderate if descending, strenuous if ascending
Elevation change: 1,750 feet
USGS quadrant: Shining Rock
Access: There are two trailheads for the Greasy Cove Trail.
The western trailhead is at a sharp bend in the road
on the Graveyard Ridge Trail 0.3 mile east of Ivestor
Gap (N 20' 41", W 51' 43"); the western end of the
trail can be reached from the Art Loeb Trail via the Art
Loeb/Greasy Cove Connector Trail. The eastern
trailhead is on the opposite (western) side of the river
from the junction of the Bridges Camp Gap Trail and
the Big East Fork Trail just south of the confluence of
Greasy Cove Prong and the Big East Fork of the
Pigeon River (N 20' 13", W 49' 37"). See maps on
pages 40–41.

There has always been some confusion as to whether this trail should be named "Greasy Cove" or "Grassy Cove." According to most maps, the ridge is "Grassy" and the prong is "Greasy." The source of this confusion has been lost over the years.

From the trailhead off the Graveyard Ridge Trail, the narrow trail bends to the north and passes a good spring after 0.3 mile. A hundred yards later, it comes to a grassy clearing and a campsite in a small saddle; a wooden sign to the left indicates the junction with the Art Loeb/Greasy Cove Connector Trail (N 21' 54", W 51' 31"). Continue along the easy path to the right, just south of the ridge top, through grass, goldenrod, blackberry, and other bramble. The trail veers to the right after 0.7 mile and begins a moderate-to-strenuous descent through a young forest along a narrow, grass-lined trail. The trail levels off at 1 mile beneath a high canopy of rhododendron and passes through acres of hay-scented fern, grasses, and sedges. A quarter-mile later, it begins a short, moderate descent to a splendid saddle where a marvelous campsite sits beneath an ancient red maple (N 20' 53", W 50' 44"). After cresting a small knob at 1.5 miles, the trail descends to another hilltop meadow and a perfect campsite. Beyond the campsite, it descends sharply to the right and approaches a spring 100 yards later; if you're looking for water, however, you should go another 100 yards downstream, where there is a much deeper pool at a confluence with another spring. From the pool, the descent is moderate to strenuous. The branch alongside the trail flows into another branch 0.3 mile later, where there is a small waterfall and a good fishing hole. The trail makes a sharp right turn at 2.4 miles, marked by an orange piece of tape on a fallen tree. It crosses Greasy Cove Prong at a small sliding rock with a deep swimming hole. On the other side of the prong, the trail may be difficult to find, since the orange tape is obscured by debris. From here, you will begin a moderate-to-strenuous descent toward the Big East Fork through dog-hobble, Eastern hemlock, and striped maple. A quarter-mile later, you will reach a small spring on the right. To the left are a large cascade and a magnificent swimming hole. The trail ends after 3.2 miles at a large campsite 50 yards upstream from the confluence of Greasy Cove Prong and the Big East Fork of the Pigeon River (N 20' 13", W 49' 37"). Coming from any other direction, this junction is hard to find, as there is little marking the trailhead except an easily overlooked piece of orange tape hanging from a yellow birch. Directly across the river are a much smaller campsite and the trailheads for the

Big East Forks Trail and the Bridges Camp Gap Trail (N 20' 13", W 49' 36").

Four highly recommended loops that begin at the Black Balsam Parking Area range from short and simple strolls to full-day hikes.

BLACK BALSAM LOOP #1
Length: 2.4 miles round trip
Difficulty: easy
Elevation change: 400 feet
USGS quadrant: Sam Knob

This simple, short hike leads through grassy balds and Northern hardwood forests. You will descend from the Black Balsam Parking Area down the Sam Knob Trail. At the trail's end, you will cross Flat Laurel Creek, turn left on the Flat Laurel Creek Trail, and loop back to the starting point.

BLACK BALSAM LOOP #2
Length: 5.3 miles round trip
Difficulty: easy to moderate
Elevation change: 560 feet
USGS quadrant: Sam Knob

This is an excellent half-day hike through a high-elevation heath bald and the early succession stages of a spruce/fir forest. You will have a spectacular view of Sam Knob, Mount Hardy, Middle Prong, and the Davidson River Valley and enjoy lots of wildflowers in a rare, fragile ecosystem.

You will descend from the Black Balsam Parking Area down the Sam Knob Trail. At the trail's end, turn left on the Flat Laurel

Creek Trail. Take the Flat Laurel Creek Trail to the Little Sam Knob Trail. At the trail's end, turn left on Mountains-to-Sea Trail I and follow it back to the paved road.

BLACK BALSAM LOOP #3

Length: 8.9 miles or 6.5 miles round trip
Difficulty: easy to moderate
Elevation change: 720 feet
USGS quadrant: Sam Knob

This is a truly superb figure-eight hike through a high-elevation heath bald, Northern hardwood forests, and various stages of a spruce/fir forest. It offers spectacular views of Sam Knob, Mount Hardy, Middle Prong Wilderness Area, Devil's Courthouse, and several waterfalls in a rare, fragile ecosystem.

Begin by taking the Sam Knob Trail down to Flat Laurel Creek, then turn left on the Flat Laurel Creek Trail. Take the Flat Laurel Creek Trail to the Little Sam Knob Trail and turn right. At the end of the Little Sam Knob Trail, turn right on the Mountains-to-Sea Trail II. Follow it to N.C. 215; however, it is *highly* recommended that you take the 0.5 mile detour to the top of Devil's Courthouse, where you will find unparalleled views of four different states. At N.C. 215, turn right and walk down the road to the trailhead for the Flat Laurel Creek Trail. The Flat Laurel Creek Trail will take you back to the Black Balsam Knob Parking Area.

Note: If you want a shorter version of this hike, begin at the trailhead for the Flat Laurel Creek Trail on N.C. 215 and omit the 2.4 miles that make up the figure eight. The hike will then total 6.5 miles.

BLACK BALSAM LOOP #4

Length: 5.1 miles or 8.9 miles round trip
Difficulty: easy to moderate
Elevation change: 550 feet
USGS quadrants: Sam Knob, Shining Rock

This hike offers spectacular views from the summits of Black Balsam Knob and Tennent Mountain. Take the Ivestor Gap Trail to Ivestor Gap, then turn right on the Art Loeb Trail III. Follow the Art Loeb Trail III back to the paved road, then turn right and return to the Black Balsam Parking Area.

Note: You can extend this hike to a full-day, highly recommended 8.9-mile loop by taking the Ivestor Gap Trail all the way to Shining Rock Gap and then returning on the Art Loeb Trail III.

GRAVEYARD FIELDS TRAIL (#64)

Length: 3.2 miles round trip
Difficulty: easy
Elevation change: 400 feet
USGS quadrant: Shining Rock
Access: Turn into the Graveyard Fields Overlook Parking Lot at Milepost 418.8 on the Blue Ridge Parkway (N 19' 12", W 50' 51"). See map on page 32.

This trail is deservedly popular. Unfortunately, it is too popular. It is heavily eroded, and the campsites are always full. Please follow the main trail and avoid hiking in the rain, so as to lessen the erosion, or give yourself—and the annually ravaged blueberry bushes—a break and visit another trail.

The blue-blazed trail begins at the right end of the parking lot down a large wooden staircase. It crosses Yellowstone Prong

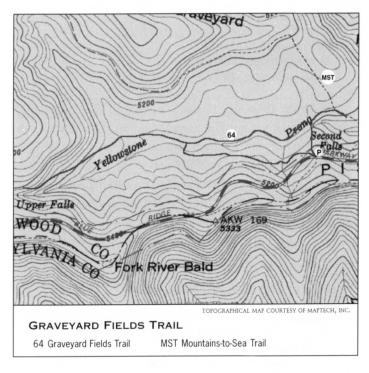

TOPOGRAPHICAL MAP COURTESY OF MAPTECH, INC.

GRAVEYARD FIELDS TRAIL

64 Graveyard Fields Trail   MST Mountains-to-Sea Trail

at 0.2 mile and reaches a trail junction marked by two carsonite signs. To the left, the trail continues upstream to Upper Falls; straight ahead, it continues to Second Falls and the Mountains-to-Sea Trail.

If you continue straight ahead at this point, you will soon bear to the right. There is a concrete post 0.1 mile later marking the junction of the Mountains-to-Sea Trail and the Second Falls Trail. The Mountains-to-Sea Trail continues straight ahead, down to Skinny Dip Falls and Bridges Camp Gap. You will turn to the right, then veer left after 20 feet and descend on a large wooden staircase to the base of the scenic cascade.

If you turn left at the first trail junction, you will follow blue blazes on the rocks for 20 yards, then veer to the right. After 1 mile, the trail forks at a carsonite sign. The trail to the left is the loop back to the parking lot; the trail straight ahead goes to the Upper Falls. You will come to a large clearing full of red maple, yellow birch, and fire cherry at 1.3 miles; hereafter, the ascent becomes moderate. A small spur trail descends to the left at a carsonite sign at 1.5 mile. A tenth of a mile later, the trail reaches the base of the spectacular Upper Falls. From the falls, backtrack 0.8 mile to the last trail junction, then turn right on the loop trail, which crosses Yellowstone Prong on a sketchy-looking but perfectly safe bridge after 50 feet, then veers to the left. From here, it is an easy hike along the southern bank of Yellowstone Prong through lots of rhododendron, opposite-leaved dogwood, galax, hay-scented fern, sedge, Carolina hemlock, willow, viburnum, St.-John's-wort, yarrow, and wood betony. About 0.5 mile past the bridge, the trail follows a long wooden walkway just before returning to the parking lot beneath a sweeping canopy of mountain laurel.

The round trip, including both waterfalls, is 3.2 miles.

Length: 4.1 miles one way
Difficulty: moderate to strenuous
Elevation change: 2,400 feet
USGS quadrant: Shining Rock
Access: From U.S. 276, turn into the parking lot on the
    western side of the road 3 miles north of the junction
    with the Blue Ridge Parkway; the parking lot is on the
    left if you are descending from the parkway (N 35°
    21' 56", W 82° 39' 6"). There is no trail sign here—
    only a wooden Forest Service board. The western
    terminus of the trail is on the Art Loeb Trail 50 yards
    south of Shining Rock Gap (N 21' 48", W 51' 50"). See
    maps on pages 40–41.

The trail begins high above the Big East Fork of the Pigeon River along an easy, narrow path of buckeye, locust, and meadow parsnip. For the first 0.3 mile, numerous spur trails to the left descend to the river; there are campsites along these spur trails. The trail forks to the right at 0.3 mile; the abandoned trail to the left goes to the Big East Fork Trail. After the fork, you will make a moderate ascent along a series of switchbacks beneath Eastern hemlock and rhododendron. A tenth of a mile later, the trail crosses a small fold where a spur trail descends steeply to the right. The trail bends to the right around a ridge line at 0.7 mile and reaches Shining Creek Gap (N 21'30", W 49'15"). The Old Butt Knob Trail begins to the right; there is no marker for this junction, so it is easily missed. You should look for a sharp bend in the trail with lots of rhododendron to the right and mountain laurel to the left. The Old Butt Knob Trail begins an immediate steep ascent to the right.

To continue on the Shining Creek Trail, go straight ahead

beneath a dense canopy of rhododendron and mountain laurel; columbine, Christmas fern, dog-hobble, erect trillium, and liverwort are present in abundance. The trail descends to Shining Creek after 0.9 mile. The creek is narrow but high in volume; a protected wild trout creek, it has copious cascades and small pools. A hundred yards across the creek is a good campsite surrounded by houstonia. Bell Collar Cove Branch cascades down a mossy rock into Shining Creek on the opposite side of the valley at 1.6 mile (N 21' 24", W 50' 2"); there is a decent swimming hole here. A large campsite is located downhill to the left 0.2 mile later; there is an excellent swimming hole 100 yards upstream from the campsite. After 2 miles, Daniels Cove Branch cascades in from the right; to the right, a small spur trail runs up the cove. Several fallen trees have formed a natural dam here, which in turn has created a large trout hole; you may see nine-inch native trout and seven-inch salamanders in this pool. A small campsite is to the left at 2.2 miles. Fifty yards later, the trail veers to the right and begins a moderate ascent alongside dozens of wake-robin trillium and umbrella-leaf. The trail switches back away from the creek as it crosses a gulch at 2.6 miles. A tenth of a mile later, the trail forks off to the right; a very large campsite is to the left beneath lots of yellow buckeye and flame azalea. Dina Branch merges with the North Prong of Shining Creek at 3 miles; at the confluence is a 50-foot-high sliding rock beneath red spruce (N 21' 44", W 51' 9"). A tenth of a mile after the confluence, you will cross the headwaters of the North Prong of Shining Creek; you may see several pinkshell azalea upstream, to your right. A tenth of a mile later, the trail bends sharply to the right and begins a long series of switchbacks. The first switchback is easily missed; look for the small cairn beneath a large red spruce. You may find wild ginger along the switchbacks. A small campsite surrounded by mossy rocks sits on a ledge at 3.6 miles. Fifty yards later, you will reach another campsite, this one with a large, cube-shaped rock in the middle. Grouse are common in this area. After a long series of mellow switchbacks, the trail crosses a boggy spring at 4 miles on old logs among Pierus, Fraser fir, red spruce, hay-scented fern, foamflower, rhododendron, and mountain laurel; if you turn around at this point, you will enjoy a nice view of Dog Loser Knob to your left at 45° and 0.7 mile. After passing through a stunning, pure stand of red spruce 0.1 mile later, you will reach the western terminus of the Shining Creek Trail at the intersection with the Art Loeb Trail (N 21' 48", W 51' 50").

It can be difficult to find this trailhead from the Art Loeb Trail. Beginning at the Shining Rock Gap intersection, you should proceed southward along the Art Loeb Trail. After 50 yards, you will reach two small spur trails on the left (east); take the *second* of the two trails, which leads into the red spruce grove. The Shining Creek Trail begins on the far right of the grove just past a small spring. For the next mile, the trail is difficult to follow because of the frequent switchbacks.

OLD BUTT KNOB TRAIL (#100)

Length: 3.6 miles one way

Difficulty: very strenuous for the first 1.5 miles, moderate
thereafter

Elevation change: 2,580 feet

USGS quadrant: Shining Rock

Access: From U.S. 276, turn into the parking lot on the
western side of the road 3 miles north of the junction
with the Blue Ridge Parkway; the parking lot is on the
left if you are descending from the parkway. There is
no trail sign here—only a wooden Forest Service
board. Follow the first paragraph of the directions for
the Shining Creek Trail, to where the Old Butt Knob
Trail forks off to the right (N 21' 30", W 49' 15"). The
western terminus of the trail is at Shining Rock Gap (N
21' 52", W 51' 59"). See maps on pages 40–41.

At Shining Creek Gap, the Old Butt Knob Trail begins a steep ascent sharply to the right along a narrow trail lined with galax, mountain laurel, and rhododendron. It quickly becomes very strenuous as it ascends Chestnut Ridge through brushy locust, flame azalea, and beech. Around 0.5 mile, just after the trail crosses a large rock, you will see a rock outcropping to the left that offers spectacular views of Shining Creek Valley (N 21' 43", W 49' 38"). To the right (northern) side of the trail is a clear view of Mount Pisgah. Just past this outcropping, the trail levels off for 30 yards, offering a welcome respite from the strenuous ascent. The trail begins a series of five or six switchbacks at 0.7 mile. A quarter-mile later, you will reach a good campsite (N 21' 53", W 49' 54") that signals the end of the difficult ascent. From here, the easy ascent leads through lots of lousewort, galax, mountain laurel, rhododendron, red maple, red spruce, and pink lady's-slipper. There is a good campsite at the crest of Chestnut Ridge at 1.5 miles (N 22' 7", W 52' 16"). The spur trail that breaks off to the left 0.3 mile later offers incredible views of Shining Rock Wilderness Area (N 22' 13", W 50' 28"); on a clear day, you can see Looking Glass Rock far to the left at 153° and 5.3 miles. At 1.9 miles, you will reach a small campsite in a grassy clearing with lots of crested dwarf iris. The trail crests Old Butt Knob at 2 miles (N 22' 18", W 50' 36"), then descends to the right. At 2.3 miles, you will reach Spanish Oak Gap, where you will find an outstanding, large campsite beneath red spruce and Fraser fir in a grassy meadow of blueberry, wake-robin trillium, yellow bead lily, and blackberry (N 20' 13", W 50' 47"). One hundred yards later, you will begin a moderate ascent to the summit of Dog Loser Knob at 2.8 miles (N 22' 12", W 51' 12"). At the summit, the trail forks to the left and passes a nice campsite on a grassy hillside looking south-southwest; a second small campsite is located 0.1 mile down the trail. A hundred yards later, you will descend into Beech Spring Gap, a bucolic, grassy meadow containing lots of Pierus and fire cherry. To find the spring, continue on the trail 50 yards past the bottom of the saddle; the spring is downhill to the left beneath yellow birch and yellow buckeye and among St.-John's-wort, hay-scented fern, and cinnamon fern (N 22' 6", W 51' 24"). As you ascend out of Beech Spring Gap up the eastern side of Shining Rock, you will pass through a beautiful, pure stand of beech and begin a moderate ascent along a series of switchbacks. A small trail breaks off to the left at 3.3 miles. Fifty yards later, the trail forks. The trail to the right heads toward the summit of Shining Rock (5,940 feet) and leads past an overused, grassy campsite to the right; it offers a nice view of Mount Pisgah to the northeast but peters out after 0.25 mile. To the left, you will see an abandoned section of trail and a wooden sign reading, "Trail closed due to erosion" (N 22' 1", W 51' 45"). From here, you will turn to the left, pass to the right of the abandoned trail, and descend to Shining Rock Gap at 3.6 miles (N 21' 52", W 51' 49").

BIG EAST FORK TRAIL (#14)

Length: 3.4 miles one way
Difficulty: moderate
Elevation change: 650 feet
USGS quadrant: Shining Rock
Access: On U.S. 276, there is a small, paved pullout on the western side of the highway 2.9 miles north of the junction with the Blue Ridge Parkway; the pullout is on the left if you are descending from the parkway. You can park here or at the Big East Fork Parking Area, located 0.1 mile farther down the hill. There is a wooden trail sign at the paved pullout (N 21' 53", W 49' 4"). The southern terminus of the trail is near the confluence of Greasy Cove Prong and the Big East Fork; the trail ends at a small campsite at the junction with the Bridges Camp Gap Trail (N 20' 13", W 49' 36"); directly across the river are the trailhead for the Greasy Cove Trail and a much larger campsite. See maps on pages 40–41.

From the southern terminus, the orange-blazed Big East Fork Trail descends downstream on a narrow path lined with dog-hobble, hemlock, rhododendron, yellow birch, red and striped maple, Southern lady fern, Christmas fern, and May apple. At 0.3 mile, a steep trail descends to a good campsite on

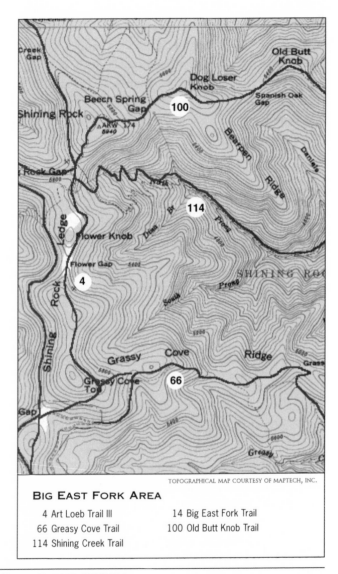

TOPOGRAPHICAL MAP COURTESY OF MAPTECH, INC.

BIG EAST FORK AREA

4 Art Loeb Trail III
66 Greasy Cove Trail
114 Shining Creek Trail

14 Big East Fork Trail
100 Old Butt Knob Trail

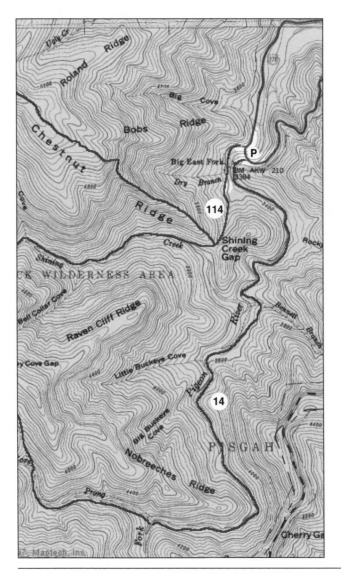

Ferns are a common sight in the Pisgah National Forest.

the left. The river makes a sharp bend to the left at 0.6 mile; the trail descends to the river. You will walk alongside the river atop exposed bedrock, then veer off to the right. At 1 mile, there is a campsite on the left with a good swimming hole. After another 0.25 mile, you will reach another, smaller campsite. Just after crossing a small bog at 1.7 miles, you will reach an excellent campsite on the right; to the left, Little Buckeye Cove Branch flows into the Big East Fork. A tenth of a mile later, the trail forks. Take the right fork; you will soon cross a small spring. The trail crosses Bennett Branch after 2.2 miles. Fifty yards later, it switches back and descends to the river; keep your eye out for the piece of orange tape. Shining Creek flows into the Big East Fork at 2.3 miles, where you'll find an excellent campsite and a truly massive swimming hole (N 21'

15", W 49' 6"). Farther downstream, the river bends sharply to the left and the trail passes briefly alongside it. The trail bends sharply to the right at 2.6 miles. Look for a small piece of orange tape on a red maple; an old footpath continues ahead. From here, you'll ascend to the right into Rocky Cove and cross a small branch among tulip poplar. A quarter-mile later, the trail descends to the river and a small wooden sign marked "Trail"; a good campsite is to the right, and several excellent swimming holes are to the left. Stairs descend to a very large campsite at 3.4 miles; just beyond the top of the stairs is a weathered, old Shining Rock sign. The trail ends 100 yards later on the western side of U.S. 276 south of the Big East Fork River.

There are two incredible full-day hikes from the Big East Fork Parking Area.

BIG EAST FORK LOOP #1
Length: 8.4 miles round trip
Difficulty: strenuous
Elevation change: 2,600 feet
USGS quadrant: Shining Rock

From the Big East Fork Parking Area, take the Old Butt Knob Trail to Shining Rock. At the trail's end, turn left on to the Art Loeb Trail and descend to Shining Rock Gap. Fifty yards past Shining Rock Gap, you will reach the Shining Creek Trail in a grove of red spruce to your left. You should then descend the Shining Creek Trail back to the parking lot.

BIG EAST FORK LOOP #2

Length: 12.2 miles round trip
Difficulty: strenuous
Elevation change: 2,600 feet
USGS quadrant: Shining Rock

From the Big East Fork Parking Area, take the Old Butt Knob Trail to Shining Rock. At the trail's end, turn left on to the Art Loeb Trail, heading south. After 1.3 miles, turn left on the Art Loeb Trail/Greasy Cove Connector Trail. It is 0.2 mile to a saddle; turn left on the Greasy Cove Trail. From here, you will descend on the Greasy Cove Trail to the Big East Fork Trail. Depending upon the season, you may have to wade the river to reach the Big East Fork Trail. Once you're on the other side, turn left on the Big East Fork Trail and return to U.S. 276 about 0.1 mile south of the Big East Fork Parking Area.

DAVIDSON RIVER VALLEY

The Davidson River Valley is a masterpiece. Flanked by Pisgah Ridge and Chestnut Ridge to the north, Shuck Ridge and Pilot Mountain to the west, and Rich Mountain, Chestnut Mountain, Chestnut Knob, and Shut-In Ridge to the south, the Davidson River snakes its way east through some of the most beautiful mountain scenery in the entire Pisgah National Forest. The valley contains some of the best waterfalls in the state, plus the highly visible Looking Glass Rock, John Rock, and Cedar Rock—three granite massifs that are reputed to be among the oldest exposed rocks on the planet. The dozens of trails here range from hikes through remote, difficult, and seldom-explored coves to easy riverside strolls at family picnic grounds. There are many waterfalls and cliffs here, but the crown jewel of the Davidson River Valley is the 17.8 miles of the Art Loeb Trail that descend from the Blue Ridge Parkway to the Davidson River on U.S. 276.

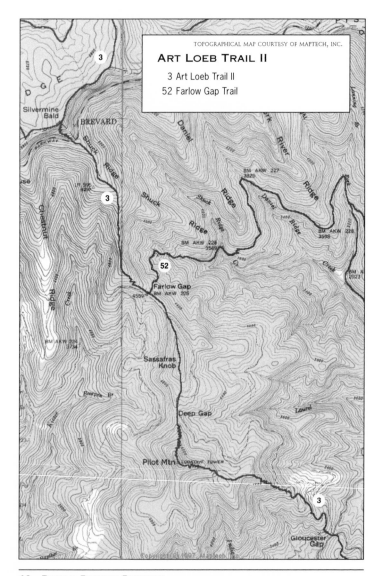

ART LOEB TRAIL II

3 Art Loeb Trail II
52 Farlow Gap Trail

ART LOEB TRAIL II

Length: 5.4 miles one way
Difficulty: strenuous
Elevation change: 2,250 feet
USGS quadrants: Sam Knob, Shining Rock
Access: The northern trailhead is located on the Blue Ridge
    Parkway 1.2 miles east of the Devil's Courthouse Parking
    Area, at Milepost 421.2 (N 35° 18' 25", W 82° 52' 52");
    there is no parking at the trailhead, so you must pull your
    car off the road and park on the grass. The southern
    trailhead, located in Gloucester Gap, is accessible from
    S.R. 1328 about 3.6 miles east of N.C. 215 (N 35° 15'
    56", W 82° 50' 48").

Note: in other maps and books, this trail is listed as being
7 miles long, rather than 5.4 miles. The reason for this discrep-
ancy is simple: we have chosen to separate the northern 1.6
miles and include them with the Mountains-to-Sea Trail I in
the Black Balsam Knob section. Unless you intend to through-
hike the entire Art Loeb Trail, there is no good reason to hike
from Silvermine Bald to the Blue Ridge Parkway or vice versa;
as far as day hikes are concerned, the best place to begin the
Art Loeb Trail II is on the parkway.

From the northern trailhead off the Blue Ridge Parkway,
the trail begins a moderate-to-strenuous descent down Shucks
Ridge through mixed hardwoods, reaching Farlow Gap (N 17'
28", W 52' 17") after 1.4 miles. At Farlow Gap, you will approach a small spur trail to the right; this is the old F.R. 140-A.
Twenty yards later, you will reach a trail hub in a large clearing;
the trail junction is marked by a carsonite sign. To the left, the
Farlow Gap Trail descends to Shuck Ridge Falls and Daniel Ridge
Trail; to the right is an old roadbed. The Art Loeb Trail continues

straight ahead to the left of the large boulder and past a good campsite. A tenth of a mile later, the old F.R. 229 veers off to the left, while the Art Loeb Trail continues straight ahead through yellow birch and witch hazel and begins a moderate-to-strenuous ascent of Sassafras Knob. You will crest Sassafras Knob at 2.2 miles. Fifty yards later, you will reach a good campsite surrounded by maidenhair fern; the campsite offers nice views to the southeast. The trail begins a series of easy-to-moderate switchbacks, descending 0.4 mile to Deep Gap. There is a large A-frame shelter in Deep Gap. To the left of the Art Loeb Trail, a spur trail descends to a spring. The Art Loeb Trail continues straight ahead, then descends to an old roadbed marked by a carsonite sign 0.1 mile later. There is another trail junction at a campsite 50 yards later; a small spur trail breaks off perpendicularly to the left, the dirt road continues straight ahead, and the Art Loeb Trail forks to the right, ascending through lots of star chickweed, houstonia, wood betony, wild hydrangea, cinnamon fern, blackberry, Turk's-cap lily, Indian pipe, rhododendron, fly poison, and clammy honeysuckle. After an endless series of strenuous switchbacks, you will reach the summit of Pilot Mountain at 3.4 miles, where you'll find copious bush honeysuckle, willow, and flame azalea, along with extensive panoramas—but no campsites. Beginning to the north, you will see Fork River Bald at 11° and 2.8 miles, Mount Pisgah at 35° and 12.2 miles, Green Knob at 37° and 6.9 miles, Rich Mountain at 53° and 7.1 miles, Looking Glass Rock at 67° and 4.6 miles, Black Mountain at 68° and 8.4 miles, John Rock at 89° and 4.3 miles, Cedar Rock at 111° and 3.9 miles, Kagle Mountain at 126° and 4.8 miles, Sassafras Mountain at 165° and 15.2

miles, Rocky Knobs at 209° and 14.7 miles, Toxaway Mountain at 218° and 11.7 miles, Bruce Knob at 240° and 3.7 miles, Rich Mountain Bald at 286° and 7.5 miles, Mount Hardy at 306° and 4 miles, Chestnut Bald at 336° and 2.6 miles, and Black Balsam Knob at 358° and 3.8 miles. The descent from Pilot Mountain follows a long series of moderate-to-strenuous switchbacks. The trail crosses a gravel road at 4.5 miles, then crosses the same road again 0.1 mile later. It switches back sharply to the left at 4.9 miles. The rock overlook to the right looks out over a sheer rock wall and a boulder field and is a perfect place for snacking. From the overlook, the trail continues a moderate descend through phacelia for almost 0.5 mile before ending at Gloucester Gap.

ART LOEB TRAIL I

Length: 12.3 miles one way
Difficulty: strenuous
Elevation change: 1,700 feet
USGS quadrants: Shining Rock, Rosman, Pisgah Forest
Access: The western trailhead is in Gloucester Gap 3.6
      miles east of N.C. 215 on S.R. 1328 (N 35° 15' 56",
      W 82° 50' 48"). The eastern trailhead is at the eastern
      end of the Art Loeb Trail Parking Area in the Davidson
      River Campground Parking Lot on U.S. 276, 1.3 miles
      north of N.C. 280 (N 35° 16' 54", W 82° 43' 14").
      See maps on pages 50–51.

From Gloucester Gap, the trail begins a short, moderate climb over Rich Mountain, then descends to F.R. 471 after 0.6 mile. Shortly thereafter, you will reach a confusing trail junction; the trail veers off to the left, following the blue dot and white dash. After a moderate-to-strenuous ascent, you will crest

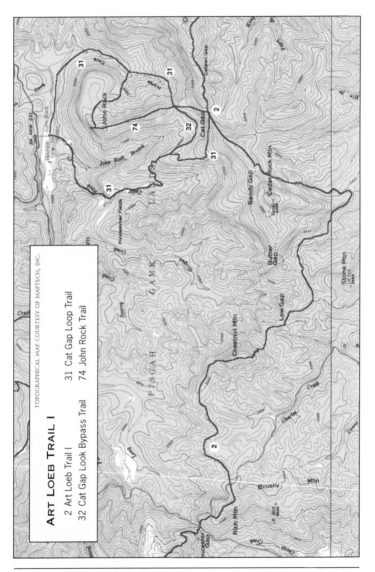

ART LOEB TRAIL I

TOPOGRAPHICAL MAP COURTESY OF MAPTECH, INC.

2 Art Loeb Trail I   31 Cat Gap Loop Trail
32 Cat Gap Look Bypass Trail 74 John Rock Trail

Chestnut Mountain and reach an excellent campsite at 2.4 miles (N 15' 38", W 49' 24"). The trail descends along a series of moderate switchbacks before reaching a small saddle and a trail junction at 3.4 miles; the Art Loeb Connector Trail begins to the left, and the main trail continues straight ahead. Almost 0.2 mile later, you will come to a major trail junction (N 15' 12", W 48' 43"). The Art Loeb Connector Trail reconnects from behind and to the left; the Butter Gap Trail descends perpendicularly to the left; an old, narrow trail begins directly across and leads 0.8 mile to Cedar Rock; and the Art Loeb Trail, marked by a wooden sign reading "Shelter," continues ahead to the right. At 3.7 miles, you will reach the Butter Gap Shelter, a large, open-faced A-frame; there is a reliable spring to your right. The trail crosses over the headwaters of Kuykendall Creek 1 mile later. Just beyond the creek, it begins the strenuous ascent of the southeastern side of Cedar Rock. After 0.2 mile, you will crest a ridge line to the right of the cliffs (N 15' 17", W 47' 55"). Almost 0.25 mile later, you will reach a large campsite to the right where there is lots of bush pea. The trail ascends to Sandy Gap at 5.4 miles (N 15' 33", W 47' 47"); to the left, a red blaze on a white oak marks an old trail leading toward Cedar Rock. Leaving Sandy Gap, you will continue northeast along the ridge line for 0.4 mile. The trail descends to Cat Gap (N 15' 53", W 47' 21") at 6 miles, where there are several trail junctions. Behind and to the left, the Cat Gap Loop Trail descends toward Cedar Rock Creek; ahead and to the right, an unnamed trail descends toward King Creek; and farther ahead and to the left, the eastern half of the Cat Gap Loop Trail descends toward Horse Cove. A moderate ascent for 0.75 mile will bring you to the summit of Chestnut Knob (N 16' 1", W 46' 35"), where you'll find a small campsite beneath several hickory trees. The trail descends a wooden staircase to F.R. 475C at 7.8 miles, turns left, and then immediately forks right. You will come to a large campsite on the right after 8.5 miles, where the trail makes an easily missed sharp bend to the left. A tenth of a mile later, the North Slope Connector Trail forks off to the left (N 16' 22", W 45' 20").

The Davidson River
PHOTO BY CAROLYN SAKOWSKI

The trail continues a gradual descent for almost 0.5 mile to Neil Gap (N 16' 26", W 44' 57"), where you'll see a peculiar but colorful handmade sign. After a moderate-to-strenuous ascent, you will crest a knob on Shut-In Ridge at 9.4 miles. The trail then descends for 0.5 mile to F.R. 5062, turns right, forks left, and continues the moderate descent on Shut-In Ridge through rattlesnake plantain, pipsissewa, partridgeberry, rhododendron, trillium, doll's eye, and lion's foot. It reaches the Davidson River Valley at 11.5 miles. From here, you will cross a wooden footbridge and meander through a hemlock grove with lots of bee balm, spiderwort, rue anemone, oxalis, cinquefoil, hawthorn, and holly. After 0.5 mile, the trail comes to a swinging bridge over the

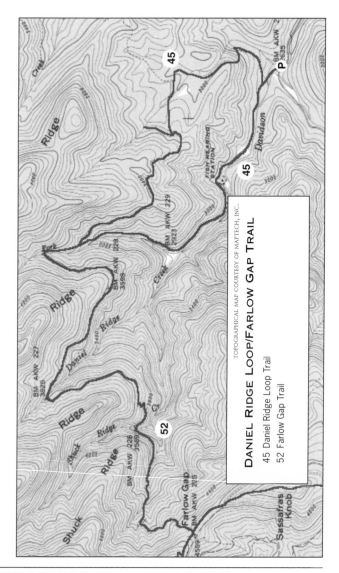

TOPOGRAPHICAL MAP COURTESY OF MAPTECH, INC.

DANIEL RIDGE LOOP/FARLOW GAP TRAIL

45 Daniel Ridge Loop Trail

52 Farlow Gap Trail

Davidson River. On the other side of the river, the Art Loeb Trail veers left and the Mountains-to-Sea Trail Alternate crosses the road to the right. Two tenths of a mile later, the Art Loeb Trail ends behind a gate at the eastern end of a small parking lot.

DANIEL RIDGE LOOP TRAIL (#45)
Length: 4 miles round trip
Difficulty: easy to moderate
Elevation change: 750 feet
USGS quadrangle: Shining Rock
Access: From U.S. 276, turn left on Pisgah Fish Hatchery Road 5.4 miles north of Brevard. Drive 4 miles to the parking area on the right; the parking area is 0.7 mile past the Cove Creek sign. The trail begins behind a gate on an old gravel road (N 35° 17' 5", W 82° 49' 43").

The red-blazed trail follows the gravel road for the first 0.1 mile, then forks left at a carsonite sign. You will make an easy ascent past several campsites along a wide gravel path lined with hemlock, rhododendron, beech, birch, dog-hobble, and poison ivy in a typical acidic cove forest. The trail forks at 0.7 mile (N 17' 20", W 50' 18"). The main trail continues straight ahead; to the left, an alternate route follows the creek. The two trails reconnect 0.6 mile later at the site of an old bridge, where only an impressive stone wall stands today (N 17' 32", W 50' 42"). Past the stone wall, the trail bends to the right, passes a small waterfall on the left, and begins a moderate ascent through columbine, various ferns, bloodroot, and trillium alongside the Right Fork of Daniel Ridge Creek. A small campsite is downhill to the left at 1.7 miles and another one is to the right 100 yards later. At 1.9 miles, you will reach a trail junction marked by a carsonite sign at the end of the ascent. The Farlow Gap Trail begins to the left; the Daniel Ridge Trail continues to the right (N 18' 2", W 50' 44"). There is another trail junction 100 yards later; follow the red blaze and veer off to the left. The trail continues eastward through opposite-leaved dogwood, Carolina silverbell, occasional spruce, and blueberry. It wraps around a ridge line at 2.4 miles, where a spur trail breaks off to the left (N 17' 40", W 50' 27"). This 0.1-mile trail connects to a grass-covered gravel road; a piece of orange tape on a young tulip poplar marks the trail's end just past a sharp bend in the road (N 17' 45", W 50' 25"). Past the junction, the trail descends along an old clay roadbed that offers nice views of Pilot Mountain to the southwest. It crosses F.R. 5046 at 3 miles (N 17' 34", W 50' 5"). If you hike almost 0.2 miles to your left down the road, you will come to an impressive waterfall. A low-volume stream cascades approximately 50 feet off a massive rock escarpment surrounded by wildflowers; it is *well* worth the small detour. Past the gravel road, the trail descends beneath a tight laurel canopy and crosses the stream on a wooden footbridge. The narrow footpath ends at a T intersection with F.R. 5046 at 3.8 miles; the intersection is marked by a carsonite sign. To the left 100 yards later is the spectacular Daniel Ridge Falls, which cascades over 150 feet down an enormous rock outcropping. No one seems to know why this is named Daniel Ridge Falls. Daniel Ridge is 2 miles to the west, and this isn't even Daniel Ridge Creek. Another, less-used name for the waterfall is Toms Spring Falls. The trail continues to the right along the gravel road for 0.2 mile before returning to the trailhead.

Length: 3.2 miles one way
Difficulty: moderate to the waterfall, moderate to
    strenuous thereafter
Elevation change: 1,300 feet
USGS quadrangle: Shining Rock
Access: The eastern trailhead is located on Daniel Ridge
    Loop Trail 1.9 miles north of F.R. 475 (N 18' 2", W 50'
    44"). The western trailhead is on the Art Loeb Trail II
    some 1.4 miles south of the Blue Ridge Parkway (N
    17' 28", W 52' 17"). See map on page 54.

Thirty yards from its junction with the Daniel Ridge Trail, the blue-blazed trail crosses the Right Fork of Daniel Ridge Creek on a wooden bridge. It then begins a series of easy-to-moderate switchbacks. The trail follows an old roadbed as it wraps around Fork River Ridge, where you'll see lots of mountain laurel, flame azalea, and sweet shrub and enjoy nice views of Sassafras Knob and Pilot Mountain to the southwest. At 1.2 miles, it crosses a small branch just upstream from a small waterfall. Fifty yards later, the trail crosses the Left Fork of Daniel Ridge Creek (N 18' 10", W 51' 32"); there is lots of pink lady's-slipper nearby. The trail begins a gradual descent as it wraps around Daniel Ridge, then passes by a large campsite beneath several red maple trees at 2 miles. From the campsite, it follows a moderate descent for 0.2 mile before reaching the spectacular Shuck Ridge Falls. The trail crosses the top of the falls, where a small spur trail descends steeply to the left to the base of the 25-foot-high falls and a truly serendipitous swimming hole. Past the falls, you will continue a moderate ascent through a lush, deep cove with lots of blue cohosh and umbrella-leaf, located to the left of the Left Prong of Shuck Ridge Creek. Half a mile past the falls, just beyond a long sliding rock, you will reach a small campsite to the left. A tenth of a mile later, the trail bends to the left and crosses the prong. Notice the abundance of mica alongside the trail as you approach the large campsite at 2.7 miles (N 17' 42", W 52' 12"); formerly, this campsite was the entrance to an old mica mine. From the mine site, the trail makes a strenuous ascent along an old roadbed before ending at Farlow Gap at 3.2 miles (N 17' 27", W 52' 18"); a carsonite sign marks the trail's junction with the Art Loeb Trail. To the right (north), it is 1.4 miles to the Blue Ridge Parkway; to the left (south), it is 1.2 miles to Deep Gap and the intersection with F.R. 229.

CANEY BOTTOM LOOP (#27)

Length: 4.6 miles round trip
Difficulty: easy to moderate
Elevation change: 500 feet
USGS quadrant: Shining Rock
Access: From U.S. 276, turn west on Fish Hatchery Road
   (F.R. 475) and drive 3.5 miles to a small parking area
   on the left. The trail begins on the right beside a large
   wooden sign for Cove Creek and an information sign
   (N 35° 16' 58", W 82° 49' 1").

The blue-blazed trail begins on a wide gravel road beneath Eastern hemlock, black birch, and rhododendron. You will cross Cove Creek on a footbridge after 100 yards. There is a small cascade to the right 0.2 mile later. The trail leaves the roadbed and breaks off to the left after 0.4 mile. Continuing to the right fifty yards later, you will reach a trail junction marked by a carsonite sign. The Caney Bottom Loop Trail breaks off sharply to the right; straight ahead, a path continues northwest to connect with F.R. 225. Just before the 1-mile mark, the trail forks to the right again. A carsonite sign points down and to the right, but if you are interested only in Cove Creek Falls, continue straight ahead for a few hundred yards. Fifty yards later, the trail descends to a campsite in a hemlock grove. It then makes a series of confusing turns, but there is a sequence of blue blazes to guide you; eventually, you will end up walking alongside Cane Bottom Creek.

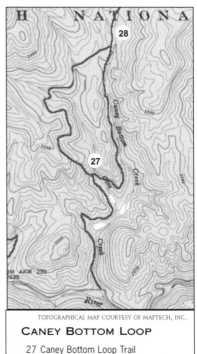

TOPOGRAPHICAL MAP COURTESY OF MAPTECH, INC.

CANEY BOTTOM LOOP

27 Caney Bottom Loop Trail
28 Caney Bottom Loop Extension Trail

After 1.4 miles, you will pass the top of a lovely slick-rock waterfall that descends nearly 70 feet into a lush, moist, and steep-walled cove. The trail crosses the creek on a wooden bridge 0.4 mile later, and again 20 yards after that. You will reach a major intersection marked by a carsonite sign at 2.1 miles. The Caney Bottom Loop Trail continues to the left; it used to continue straight ahead but was redirected. The yellow-blazed Caney Bottom Loop Extension Trail begins to the right and heads north-northwest past an excellent campsite to a road intersection after 0.75 mile. At that intersection, an old road to the left heads to Caney Creek; two old abandoned roadbeds are to the right; and the road straight ahead connects with F.R. 475B.

Follow the blue blaze across the creek to the left to continue on the Caney Bottom Loop. The trail continues west-southwest on an old roadbed. To the left of the road is a hemlock grove. To the right is an old, overgrown meadow with some wild cherry trees and lots of goldenrod. A tenth of a mile later, a spur trail marked by an old wooden signpost forks off to the left. The trail crosses the eastern prong of Cove Creek at 2.4 miles and continues an easy stroll along the ridge contour through a laurel slick. You will reach a trail junction at 2.7 miles. A yellow-blazed trail begins to the right; the main trail veers to the left and descends a wooden staircase. There is a good campsite to the left. The trail crosses Cove Creek on an exceptionally sturdy wooden footbridge. Shortly thereafter, you will cross two gulches. The trail continues a gradual descent on the old railroad grade, cut into the steep walls of the creek valley. A small spur trail, marked by a piece of yellow tape on a mountain laurel, drops to the left at 3.6 miles; the spur trail descends past a small campsite and veers to the right to the spectacular Cove Creek Falls (N 17' 38", W 49' 4"). The waterfall cascades almost 70 feet down a multitiered rock wall and eventually collects into a small bathing hole at the base. At the base of the creek on the other side of the falls are a campsite and an abandoned trail that reconnects with the Caney Bottom Loop Trail. From here, it is a couple hundred yards to the loop fork and 1 mile back to the parking lot.

LOOKING GLASS ROCK TRAIL (#86)

Length: 3.1 miles one way
Difficulty: moderate to strenuous
Elevation change: 1,600 feet
USGS quadrant: Shining Rock
Access: From U.S. 276, turn west on F.R. 475 (Fish
    Hatchery Road) 5.4 miles north of N.C. 280. Drive 0.4
    mile to the large parking area on the right. See map
    on page 62.

This is unquestionably one of the most heavily used trails in the national forest—and often the most accident prone. While it does provide some spectacular scenery, its popularity tends to diminish its beauty.

The yellow-blazed trail follows a moderate ascent through a hemlock grove in an acidic cove forest. You will ascend above a small creek for the first 0.6 mile and pass an abundance of wildflowers including spring beauty, trailing arbutus, bloodroot, trout lily, foamflower, various trilliums, iris cristata, phlox, thalictrum, chickweed, serviceberry, clintonia, oxalis, Canadian mayflower, teaberry, and many others. The trail crosses a large rock after 1 mile, where it offers a nice view to the southeast of the Davidson River Valley. Shortly thereafter, it passes beneath a thick canopy of rhododendron and begins a series of moderately difficult switchbacks; please refrain from using the old, destructive shortcuts, as they increase erosion. The trail opens up and the terrain becomes noticeably less steep after 1.8 miles. But don't be fooled into thinking that the trail is nearly over; you are still less than halfway there. About 0.5 mile later, you will reach a rock clearing with a large white **H** painted on it (N 17' 52", W 47' 20"); it is used as a helicopter pad by the

Transylvania County Rescue Squad. A spur trail breaks off to the right 0.2 mile later. This 0.4-mile detour wraps around the southeastern corner of Looking Glass Rock and offers views to the east; however, the eastern portion of the summit is closed off to protect a peregrine falcon reintroduction effort, so the trail is no longer in use. The spur rejoins the main trail from the right at 2.7 miles. Shortly thereafter, the trail begins a final strenuous ascent toward the summit. You will reach the summit of Looking Glass Rock (3,969 feet) after 3 miles. Here, you will enjoy nice views of Cedar Rock due south. To reach the

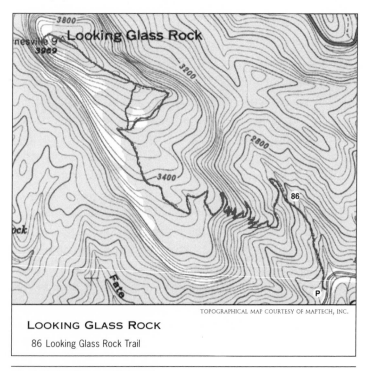

TOPOGRAPHICAL MAP COURTESY OF MAPTECH, INC.

LOOKING GLASS ROCK

86 Looking Glass Rock Trail

Looking Glass Rock from the Blue Ridge Parkway

cliffs, follow the trail as it descends a short series of switchbacks through the mountain laurel. The trail ends on the southwestern corner of Looking Glass Rock, where you'll see patches of hemlock, table mountain pine, Eastern red cedar, blueberry, and moss. Beginning at the left, you will see Cedar Rock at 190° and 3.2 miles, Three Forks Mountain at 204° and 6.2 miles, Pilot Mountain at 247° and 4.6 miles, Sassafras Knob at 257° and 4.3 miles, Tanasee Bald at 267° and 7 miles, Chestnut Bald at 276° and 5.3 miles, Fork River Bald at 285° and 3.8 miles, Black Balsam Knob at 294° and 4.7 miles, Shining Rock at 321° and 5.8 miles, Chestnut Ridge at 325° and 2.5 miles, Green Knob at 358° and 3.7 miles, Fryingpan Mountain at 15° and 6.3 miles, Mount Pisgah at 18° and 8.7 miles, Little Bald Mountain at 25° and 7.6 miles, and Buckwheat Knob at 26° and 2.2 miles.

Note: Looking Glass Rock is deceptively dangerous. The slope quickly shifts from horizontal to vertical, and there is nothing to prevent you from falling off the cliff, even if you slip at the top, where it is flat.

Mountains-to-Sea Trail

Prior to 1977, the dream of a continuous hiking trail that extended from the Great Smoky Mountains to the Outer Banks of North Carolina lived only in the imaginations of a few dedicated hikers and outdoor enthusiasts. In a speech at the 1977 National Trails Symposium, Howard N. Lee, then the secretary of the North Carolina Department of Natural Resources and Community Development (now the Department of the Environment, Health, and Natural Resources) gave the idea official sanction when he suggested that a trail from the mountains to the coast be created. Such a trail, he said, "would give North Carolinians and national visitors using it a real feel for the sights, sounds and people of the state." Since then, dedicated volunteers and state officials have made a collaborative effort to bring the dream to reality. By 2000, many portions of the trail were open, including large sections in Pisgah National Forest.

The task is formidable. In total, the Mountains-to-Sea Trail is expected to stretch 870 miles and include parts of the Blue Ridge Parkway, Pisgah National Forest, Croatan National Forest, Hanging Rock State Park, Stone Mountain State Park, Pilot Mountain State Park, Uwharrie National Forest, Bladen Lakes State Forest, the Dismal Swamp, and Cape Hatteras National Seashore. Construction of the trail is to be a cooperative effort among volunteers, state officials, and individual and corporate landowners.

Of the 380 miles planned for the western part of the state, 253.7 miles have been completed. Designated sections of the Mountains-to-Sea Trail are marked with a white circle three inches in diameter. The trail enters Pisgah National Forest at the Middle Prong Wilderness and traverses the Pisgah Ranger District. Its course roughly parallels the Blue Ridge Parkway. There are many access points to the Mountains-to-Sea Trail along the parkway. Like the parkway, the trail leaves Pisgah National Forest, passes south of Asheville, and reenters the national forest at the Great Craggy range. From there, it continues to Mount Mitchell, then passes through Linville Gorge. From the eastern rim of Linville Gorge, the trail descends to Wilson Creek, where it exits Pisgah National Forest and continues into the Piedmont region of North Carolina.

The Mountains-to-Sea Trail is far from finished. Completion will require the continued efforts of leaders and volunteers, especially in the Piedmont and coastal regions. If you would like to help, you are encouraged to contact one of the many task forces throughout the state. An excellent source of information on the project is the book entitled *The Mountains-to-Sea Trail: Western North Carolina's Majestic Rival to the Appalachian Trail*, by Donald E. Dossey and John I. Hillyer. The book contains contact information for local task forces.

CAT GAP LOOP TRAIL (#31)

Length: 4.4 miles round trip
Difficulty: moderate
Elevation change: 1,000 feet
USGS quadrant: Shining Rock
Access: The trail is located at the Visitor Center Parking
    Area for the Pisgah National Forest Fish Hatchery on
    the Davidson River. To reach the parking area, turn off
    U.S. 276 on to Davidson River Road (F.R. 475) 5.4
    miles north of the junction with N.C. 280. The Fish
    Hatchery Parking Lot is on the left 1.5 miles down the
    road, just before the pavement ends. The Cat Gap
    Loop Trail has two trailheads. One is located at the far
    left (eastern) end of the parking lot, and the other is
    behind a gate near the visitor center (N 35° 17' 2", W
    82° 47' 28"). See map on page 68.

From the eastern trailhead, the orange-blazed trail begins alongside the Davidson River on a wide, old roadbed. You will cross Cedar Rock Creek and continue along the Davidson River, then leave the river and walk southward along Horse Cove Creek through hemlock, hawthorn, rhododendron, mountain laurel, dog-hobble, lady fern, Christmas fern, foamflower, pipsissewa, rattlesnake plantain, rue anemone, various violets, phacelia, cinquefoil, poison ivy, and club moss. After 0.75 mile, the trail rock-hops West Horse Cove Creek beside meadow rue, black cohosh, maidenhair fern, partridgeberry, houstonia, and trout lily. The trail begins a moderate ascent. Fifty yards later, it crosses F.R. 475C. From here, it leaves the old roadbed and continues straight ahead up Horse Cove through a tulip poplar grove where you'll see dogwood, redbud, flame azalea, wild hydrangea, blue cohosh, crane-fly orchid, wild geranium, oxalis, star chickweed, and crested dwarf iris. At 1.3 miles, you will pass a carsonite sign and a trail junction; the John Rock Trail begins to the right. At 1.9 miles, the trail reaches a saddle at Horse Cove Gap (N 16' 8", W 47' 17"), where there are two trail junctions. The John Rock Trail begins to the far right; the Cat Gap Loop Bypass Trail begins straight ahead; and the Cat Gap Loop Trail continues to the left. You will negotiate a moderate-to-strenuous ascent as you continue along the ridge to Cat Gap at 2.2 miles, where the Cat Gap Loop Trail intersects the Art Loeb Trail and overlaps it to the right for 10 yards before forking to the right at a carsonite sign. The decent is easy to moderate as you continue through various genera of heath on a beautiful, spacious ridge side. The Cat Gap Loop Bypass Trail reconnects from the right at a T intersection at 2.8 miles (N 16' 9", W 47' 41"). You will follow a moderate descent for the next 0.5 mile before crossing a creek at 3.3 miles. Thirty yards past the creek, there is an excellent campsite in a large grove of white pine. You will cross the creek again 0.2 mile later. Beyond the creek, the forest canopy dies back and the trail passes through an open, flat meadow with lots of ironweed, goldenrod, blackberry, cinnamon fern, spicebush, and cherry. You will pass several spur trails leading to campsites just before you cross Grogan Creek at 3.8 miles. Twenty yards later, the Buter Gap Trail forks off to the left at a large rock, while the Cat Gap Loop Trail goes straight ahead past a nice cascade and an exquisite campsite. The trail continues a gradual descent on a sandy roadbed beneath a canopy of mountain laurel before reaching a gravel road at 4.4 miles. From here, you will cross Cedar Rock Creek on a wooden

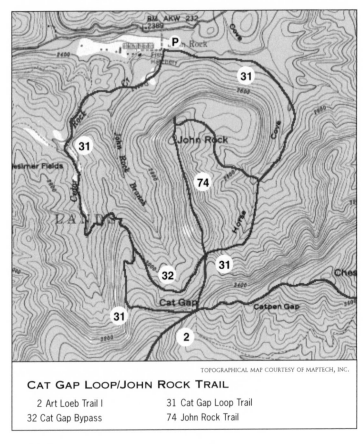

TOPOGRAPHICAL MAP COURTESY OF MAPTECH, INC.

CAT GAP LOOP/JOHN ROCK TRAIL

2 Art Loeb Trail I	31 Cat Gap Loop Trail
32 Cat Gap Bypass	74 John Rock Trail

footbridge and walk alongside a fence through a hemlock grove before returning to the parking area 0.3 mile later.

CAT GAP LOOP BYPASS TRAIL

Length: 0.6 mile one way
Difficulty: easy
Elevation change: 100 feet
USGS quadrant: Shining Rock

The Cat Gap Loop Bypass Trail is a simple, short, and sublime hike. It reduces the Cat Gap Loop Trail by a little more than 0.3 mile in distance and 250 feet in elevation gain, bypassing the most strenuous section of the Cat Gap Loop.

The trail begins in Horse Cove Gap (N 35° 16' 8", W 82° 47' 17") and gradually descends to the west. You will follow the horseshoe contour of the land as you wrap around the small cove of John Rock Creek. The terrain is spacious and gentle beneath an open, beautiful canopy of hemlock and large hardwoods. The trail reconnects with the Cat Gap Loop Trail 0.6 mile later (N 35° 16' 9", W 82° 47' 41").

JOHN ROCK TRAIL (#74)

Length: 1.8 miles one way
Difficulty: moderate to strenuous
Elevation change: 720 feet
USGS quadrant: Shining Rock
Access: The two trailheads for the John Rock Trail are both
      on the Cat Gap Loop Trail. One is located in Horse
      Cove Gap (N 35° 16' 8", W 82° 47' 17") 1.9 miles
      from the Fish Hatchery Parking Lot. The other is near
      Horse Cove Creek (N 35° 16' 28", W 82° 46' 59") 1.3
      miles from the same parking lot.

From the trailhead in Horse Cove Gap, you will follow a moderate-to-strenuous ascent along a well-worn path for the first 0.2 mile. After that, the trail reaches a good campsite at the

View of John Rock as seen from Looking Glass

ridge top. From there, it begins a series of moderate ascents and descents as it winds north toward the cliffs. The small spur trail that breaks off to the left at 0.6 mile goes to a small campsite beneath three chestnut oaks. A hundred yards later, the trail forks again. The right fork is the continuation of the John Rock Trail; the left fork is a 20-yard spur trail to the cliffs. Amidst mountain laurel, rhododendron, blueberry, Eastern hemlock, and pitch pine, the mountainside opens up to an enormous rock exposure that looks out over the Davidson River at Pisgah Ridge and the Blue Ridge Parkway. You will see the fish hatchery directly beneath you, Looking Glass Rock directly in front, Pilot Mountain at 269° and 4.4 miles, Chestnut Bald at 293° and 5.9 miles, Fork River Bald at 306° and 4.7 miles, Black Balsam Knob at 310° and 5.8 miles, Chestnut Ridge at 338° and 4 miles, Green

Knob at 358° and 5.4 miles, Fryingpan Mountain at 11° and 7.9 miles, Little Bald Mountain at 20° and 9.2 miles, Coontree Mountain at 38° and 2.6 miles, and Black Mountain at 47° and 4.6 miles.

From the cliffs, the trail descends to a small spring after 0.2 mile and passes a few good campsites. You will hike alongside the branch for 0.2 mile before crossing it. Soon thereafter, the trail reconnects with the Cat Gap Loop Trail in Horse Cove.

COONTREE LOOP (#41)

Length: 3.7 miles round trip
Difficulty: moderate
Elevation change: 1,200 feet
USGS quadrant: Shining Rock
Access: Park at the Coontree Picnic Area (N 35° 17' 23",
    W 82° 42' 43"), located on the western side of U.S.
    276 some 4.9 miles north of N.C. 280. The trail
    begins on the other side of the road. See maps on
    pages 76–77.

The blue-blazed trail begins on an easy, wide footpath to the right of Coontree Creek. It forks by an old wooden post and two carsonite signs almost 0.2 mile later. If you take the left fork, you will begin an easy-to-moderate ascent through hawthorn, wild geranium, cinquefoil, lobelia, turtlehead, hemlock, and black birch in a wide, gently sloping valley. This trail is particularly nice in the afternoon, as the setting sun casts a golden glow on the hillside to the right. After 0.75 mile, the trail bends to the right and crosses a footbridge. There is a confusing intersection 0.2 mile later, marked by an old sign nailed to a young tulip poplar. An old trail continues straight ahead;

the Coontree Loop veers off to the left. At 1.2 miles, the trail makes another sharp switchback to the left, marked by a double blue dot on a beech. From here, you will begin a series of strenuous switchbacks up the ridge side. At 1.8 miles, the trail intersects the Bennett Gap Trail just southeast of the summit of Coontree Mountain; the intersection is marked by a red-and-blue blaze on an old white oak (N 18' 32", W 45' 43"). For those interested in lengthening the hike, there are two spectacular overlooks to the left. Just prior to 0.7 mile, the first overlook will be on your right. It looks out over the entire Avery Creek Valley. The second overlook descends to the left about fifty yards later and looks out across the Davidson River Valley. The 1.4-mile round trip is well worth the time and energy. For the next 0.5 mile, the trails overlap as they descend the ridge line to Coontree Gap. At Coontree Gap (N 18' 13", W 45' 18"), the Bennett Gap Trail forks off to the right and the Coontree Loop switches down to the right. You will cross the creek after 2.6 miles; an old trail marked by an old trail sign climbs to the right, but the Coontree Loop continues to the left on an old roadbed beneath a grove of young hemlock. It crosses the creek on a wooden footbridge at 3.5 miles just before reconnecting with the other end of the loop.

AVERY CREEK AREA

To the northeast of the Davidson River lies the Avery Creek Valley. Avery Creek begins just south of Club Gap and descends 1,200 feet in 5 miles before flowing into the Davidson River. It is enclosed by Bearpen Mountain, Coontree Mountain, and Buckwheat Knob to the west, Rich Mountain to the north, and Clawhammer Mountain, Black Mountain, and Hickory Knob to the east.

There are numerous trails within the valley, seven of which are covered here. They range from short, simple wildflower tours to long, strenuous ridge hikes. With the exception of the Black Mountain Trail, which begins on U.S. 276, all the trails begin off F.R. 477, which begins and ends on U.S. 276.

If you are approaching from the south, take N.C. 280 to U.S. 276 in Brevard. Drive 2.1 miles north on U.S. 276 and turn right on to the dirt road, following the signs for the horse stables.

If you are approaching from the north, you can turn left on F.R. 477 some 3.7 miles south of the Blue Ridge Parkway or 0.5 mile south of Pink Beds Parking Area. However, unless you want to go to Bennett Gap, it is actually faster to continue down U.S. 276 to the southern end of the road and turn left there.

There are also several potential loop trails in Avery Creek Valley, four of which are highly recommended.

Note: Apart from an ephemeral spring near Buckhorn Gap Shelter, there is no water on this trail, so pack accordingly.

From the parking area, turn left and walk on the gravel road beside the barbed-wire fence and past the carsonite sign for the trailhead. Almost 0.2 mile later, the Black Mountain Trail leaves the road and forks to the left on a narrow footpath; the Thrift Cove Trail continues straight ahead. You will follow a moderate ascent of an old roadbed to the left of Thrift Cove Creek through hemlock, rhododendron, dog-hobble, lady fern, Christmas fern, interrupted fern, and ground cedar. The Mountains-to-Sea Trail Alternate merges in from the right after 0.5 mile; it runs conjunctively with the Black Mountain Trail for the next 6.5 miles before it breaks off and descends to the Pink Beds. The trail ascends away from the cove and reaches a dirt road at 1.4 miles (N 18' 0", W 43' 43"). The Thrift Cove Trail descends to the right; an old footpath continues straight ahead; and the Black Mountain Trail forks to the left. From here, you will begin an easy-to-moderate ascent along the ridge contour before switching back sharply to the right at a wooden sign 0.3 mile later. The trail ascends through blueberry, mountain laurel, and fly poison to the summit of Hickory Knob at 2.4 miles; the terrain levels off at the summit, where there are several good places to camp. From the summit, you will descend 0.3 mile to F.R. 5098 and a small clearing at Pressley Gap (N 18' 46", W 43' 46"). The trailhead for the Pressley Cove Trail is 0.2 mile down the gravel road to the left; the Black Mountain Trail continues straight ahead up a flight of steps and past locust, goat's-rue, black-eyed Susan, blackberry, and oak fern. There is a nice, small campsite to the left at 3.7 miles. Almost 0.25 mile later the narrow and easily missed Turkey Pen Gap Trail forks off to the right; it is marked by a carsonite sign. The Black Mountain Trail does not crest the actual summit of Black Mountain but rather skirts along the southwestern side of the peak beneath a high canopy of rhododendron. At 4.2 miles, just past the summit, you will see a campsite uphill to the right beneath a relatively large white oak. You will then descend to a small saddle and a rock outcropping at 4.4 miles, where you'll have excellent views to the west of Looking Glass Rock at 243° and 3.6 miles, Pilot Mountain at 246° and 8.3 miles, Rich Mountain at 295° and 2 miles, and Cold Mountain at 313° and 8.7 miles. Twenty yards

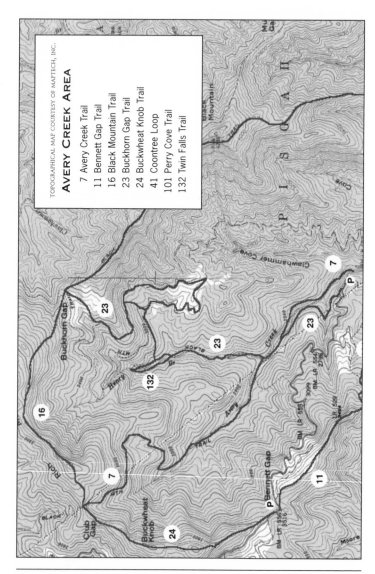

TOPOGRAPHICAL MAP COURTESY OF MAPTECH, INC.

AVERY CREEK AREA

7 Avery Creek Trail
11 Bennett Gap Trail
16 Black Mountain Trail
23 Buckhorn Gap Trail
24 Buckwheat Knob Trail
41 Coontree Loop
101 Perry Cove Trail
132 Twin Falls Trail

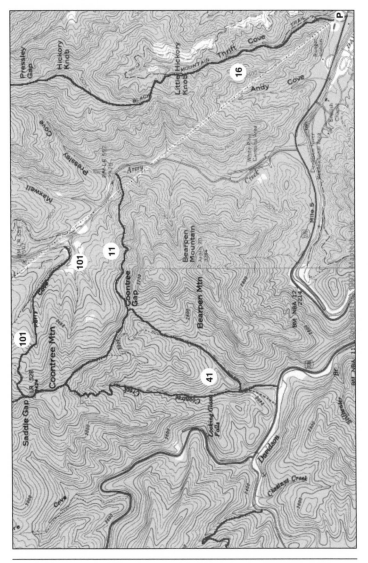

past the overlook is a large rock overhang that creates a decent shelter. You will then ascend an easy-to-moderate grade through lots of Solomon's-seal, Clinton's lily, meadow rue, phlox, and Indian cucumber before cresting Clawhammer Mountain 0.25 mile later. The trail descends to Buckhorn Gap (N 20' 30", W 45' 5") at 5.7 miles, where there are multiple trail junctions. The Buckhorn Gap Trail descends steeply to the left toward Avery Creek and to the right toward the South Mills River; a gravel road continues ahead to the left; directly across are two carsonite signs that mark the Black Mountain Trail and the Buckhorn Gap Shelter. Three tenths of a mile later, you will reach the Buckhorn Gap Shelter, an old, three-walled cabin with several bunks built into it. Leaving the shelter, you will follow a moderate-to-strenuous ascent to the crest of Soapstone Ridge, passing squaw-corn, mountain mint, and an ephemeral spring along the way. Descending from the ridge crest, you will pass a good campsite at 6.8 miles; it offers excellent views to the southwest over the Avery Creek and Davidson River Valleys. A tenth of a mile later, the trail descends to a small saddle (N 20' 44", W 45' 53"). Here, the Mountains-to-Sea Trail Alternate switches back to the right and descends to the Pink Beds. The Black Mountain Trail continues a moderate ridge walk through blue cohosh, lady's-slipper, whorled loosestrife, wood fern, and poison ivy before reaching the summit of Rich Mountain beneath a large black oak at 7.5 miles (N 20' 28", W 46' 14"). From the summit, you will begin a moderate descent of a washed-out, rocky ravine through mountain holly, dogwood, and oxalis. The trail ends by a wooden sign in Club Gap (20' 24", W 46' 30") after 7.8 miles. From here, the Avery Creek Trail descends to

Water Purification

Unfortunately, water purification is a necessity in the North Carolina Mountains. The most common water-borne illness is caused by the protozoan *Giardia lamblia*. This illness typically manifests itself in abdominal discomfort and diarrhea. *Giardia*, which causes the intestinal infection known as giardiasis, can be treated with medicines.

To avoid this and other disease-causing microorganisms, it is essential to treat surface water. There are three methods: boiling, chemical treatment, and filtering.

Water should be boiled for at least one minute. It is recommended that it be boiled for three minutes at high altitudes. Boiling takes time and requires fuel, but it kills bacteria, protozoa, and viruses.

The two chemicals commonly used in water purification are iodine and chlorine. They each have the advantage of being lightweight and compact. However, each has disadvantages. Iodine disinfection takes 30 minutes to be effective, and even longer if the water is very cold. Often, hikers become impatient and drink water that has not been optimally treated. Additionally, iodine can be toxic if consumed in large amounts. Chlorine is not reliable for killing cryptosporidium, another infectious organism that causes diarrhea. Hikers often notice a change in the taste of water after chemical treatment. Iodine and chlorine can be purchased at any outdoor store.

Water filters work fairly quickly and are lightweight and portable. Filters that have pores measuring 0.2 microns or less should catch all bacteria and protozoa. Certain purifier filters are able to eliminate viruses as well. The finer the filter, the more resistance is encountered by water passing through it—and thus the slower the operation. Reputable filters can be purchased at outdoor stores for an average cost of $50 to $90.

the left, the Buckwheat Knob Trail begins straight ahead, and the Club Gap Trail descends to the right toward the Cradle of Forestry's Forest Discovery Center.

BUCKWHEAT KNOB TRAIL (#24)

Length: 1.5 miles one way
Difficulty: moderate
Elevation change: 500 feet
USGS quadrant: Shining Rock
Access: The northern trailhead is in Club Gap (35° 20' 24", W 82° 46' 30"), accessible via the Black Mountain Trail, the Club Gap Trail, or the Avery Creek Trail. The southern trailhead is in Bennett Gap on F.R. 477 (N 35° 19' 17", W 82° 46' 31") some 2.6 miles from the western junction with U.S. 276, which is 0.5 mile south of the Pink Beds Parking Area. See maps on pages 76–77.

From the trailhead at Club Gap, the yellow-blazed trail begins an easy-to-moderate ascent past a power-line tower through lots of black cohosh. There is a campsite on the right beneath a large red maple almost 0.2 mile later. You will briefly follow a moderate ascent before the trail levels off on a serene, grassy knob with lots of crested dwarf iris and coreopsis beneath a canopy of young, mixed hardwoods. There is a great campsite to the left at 0.9 mile, just before the trail begins descending Buckwheat Knob (N 19' 46", W 46' 46"). The descent is moderate as it passes beneath several large oak trees, then becomes rather steep. The trail ends at 1.5 miles on F.R. 477. To reach the Bennett Gap Trail, turn left, go 50 yards down the dirt road, then fork to the right behind the gate.

Length: 2.9 miles one way
Difficulty: moderate if descending from Bennett Gap,
    strenuous if hiking up from Avery Creek
Elevation change: 1,200 feet
USGS quadrants: Shining Rock, Pisgah Forest
Access: Both trailheads are on F.R. 477. The northern
    trailhead is in Bennett Gap (N 35° 19' 17", W 82° 46'
    31") some 2.6 miles from the northern intersection with
    U.S. 276. The southern trailhead, located just before the
    third bridge, is 1.4 mile from the southern intersection
    with U.S. 276 (N 35° 18' 17", W 82° 44' 23"). See maps
    on pages 76–77.

From the northern trailhead in Bennett Gap, the red-blazed trail follows the road behind the gate for 20 yards before forking to the right. You will continue along a roadbed beneath a laurel slick. After 0.1 mile, the trail opens into a spacious meadow on the ridge top. At the far end of the meadow is a large campsite. Upon leaving the meadow, the trail enters a quiet hardwood forest where you'll see lots of moss, multiple fern varieties, Carolina silverbell, black birch, chinkapin, blueberry, mountain laurel, and other members of the heath family, all dripping with lichen. A short spur trail to the right at 0.7 mile descends to a small rock outcropping that offers a magnificent view of the Davidson River Valley to the southwest. From this unique angle, the cliffs of Looking Glass Rock, John Rock, and Cedar Rock are in perfect alignment. Other peaks in view are Three Forks Mountain at 213° and 7.7 miles, Chestnut Mountain at 225° and 5 miles, Toxaway Mountain at 228° and 17.7 miles, Pilot Mountain at 247° and 6.4 miles, Fork River Bald at 273° and 5.3 miles, and Green Knob at 330° and 3.4

miles. Fifty yards later, there is another excellent outcropping beneath dwarf white pine, sourwood, and pitch pine. The Avery Creek Valley is to the left, enclosed by Hickory Knob at 105° and 2.1 miles, Black Mountain at 69° and 1.9 miles, Clawhammer Mountain at 47° and 1.8 miles, and Rich Mountain at 354° and 1.8 miles. Two tenths of a mile later, the trail descends to Saddle Gap. From here, the Perry Cove Trail descends to the left. You will next ascend Coontree Mountain through galax, flame azalea, rhododendron, crested dwarf iris, and dogwood; you will pass an enormous black oak. The Coontree Loop Trail joins the trail from the right at 1.4 mile; for the next 0.6 mile, the two trails run conjunctively as they follow a moderate descent to Coontree Gap, where the Coontree Loop Trail forks off to the right. Two tenths of a mile later, the trail passes through a forest clearing that offers excellent views of Avery Creek Valley to the north; for those hiking the highly recommended 12.2-mile Avery Creek Valley Loop #3, this opening provides a clear perspective of the distance traveled. The trail continues an easy-to-moderate descent along the ridge side, then passes a spring featuring thimbleberry, maidenhair fern, meadow rue, doll's eye, and a sizable beech tree at 2.4 miles. You will pass through a young grove of hemlock before reaching a T intersection with an old roadbed 0.1 mile later. To the left, the roadbed descends deep into Perry Cove; to the right, the Bennett Gap Trail continues through sycamore, dog-hobble, rhododendron, monarda, foamflower, wild geranium, blue cohosh, rue anemone, and other wildflowers as it approaches Avery Creek. The trail ends on F.R. 477 at 2.9 miles. To the left, it is 100 yards to the Pressley Cove Trail and 0.6 mile to the

Perry Cove Trail; to the right, it is 1.4 miles to the junction with U.S. 276.

PERRY COVE TRAIL (#101)
Length: 1.2 miles one way
Difficulty: strenuous
Elevation change: 1,000 feet
USGS quadrants: Pisgah Forest, Shining Rock
Access: From U.S. 276 some 2.1 miles north of N.C. 280, turn east on to F.R. 477, following the signs for the horse stables. After 2 miles, turn left on the grassy road and park behind the gate (N 35° 18' 33", W 82° 44' 51"). See maps on pages 76–77.

The orange-blazed trail follows the dirt road for 0.1 mile, then forks to the right at a carsonite sign. You will begin a moderate ascent on an old roadbed to the right of Perry Creek through rhododendron, hemlock, oak, viburnum, Christmas fern, lady fern, helianthus, and bloodroot. The trail crosses the creek after 0.3 mile and begins a moderate-to-strenuous ascent. Two tenths of a mile later, it passes through a small but attractive meadow before entering a dense forest. You will cross a small spring after 0.6 mile. Soon thereafter, the trail begins a steep climb up Coontree Mountain. The hillside is sparsely vegetated; there is lots of open space and just a few large hardwoods. If you turn around, you will enjoy impressive views of Clawhammer Mountain, Black Mountain, and Hickory Knob. After 1 mile, you will reach the top of the hillside and come to a T intersection with an old roadbed. Note that this junction is easily missed on the return route. The trail veers to the left and makes an easy-to-moderate ascent on the roadbed, then crosses another roadbed 0.2 mile later. In the next 75 yards, the trail, badly overgrown with pokeweed and other bramble, begins a moderate-to-strenuous ascent. The last 0.1 mile is rather strenuous. The trail ends in Saddle Gap (N 18' 48", W 45' 51") at the junction with the red-blazed Bennett Gap Trail, marked by a carsonite sign. From here, it is highly recommended that you turn right on the Bennett Gap Trail; there is a wonderful overlook on the right after 0.2 mile and an even more impressive one on the left 50 yards later.

BUCKHORN GAP TRAIL (#23)

Length: 2.9 miles one way
Difficulty: moderate
Elevation change: 1,000 feet
USGS quadrant: Shining Rock
Access: From U.S. 276 some 2.1 miles north of N.C. 280, turn east on F.R. 477. Drive 2.6 miles down the dirt road. You will pass the horse stables and come to a sharp bend to the left; there is a small parking area on the right. The trail, marked by a small sign, begins to the right (N 35° 18' 56", W 82° 45' 04"). See maps on pages 76–77.

The orange-blazed trail is wide and fairly eroded for the first 0.5 mile, due largely to equestrian use. A small waterfall and a perfect swimming hole are to the right at 0.4 mile. The wooden sign after 0.8 mile indicates that the horse trail breaks off to the right, while the footpath continues to the left; behind and to the right is a sign for the Lower Avery Creek Trail (to the right) and the Upper Avery Creek Trail (the old name for this section of the Buckhorn Gap Trail). Almost 0.1 mile later, you will reach a second trail junction, marked by a wooden sign. The Avery Creek Trail forks to the left; the Buckhorn Gap Trail turns right and crosses Avery Creek (N 19' 22", W 45' 31"). From here, the trail becomes a real wildflower tour de force. It makes a sharp left past large clusters of foamflower, bluets, wood anemone, violets, trout lily, and May apple. You will cross Henry Branch 0.2 mile later; you will do so four more times over the next 0.25 mile. There is a third trail junction at 1.6 miles, marked by a carsonite sign (N 19' 54", W 45' 31"). The Twin Falls Trail descends to the left; the Buckhorn Gap Trail continues ahead. The Twin Falls Trail loops back around with the Buckhorn Gap Trail, returning to this intersection after approximately 0.6 mile; it is well worth the detour for those who plan to continue toward Buckhorn Gap. Continuing on the Buckhorn Gap Trail, you will reach a large horse circle after 0.1 mile. Here, the Buckhorn Gap Trail switches back to the right and ascends out of the valley past mountain laurel and purple-crested dwarf iris. Several hundred yards later, the trail forks to the left; it eventually merges with a wide, old roadbed. The Buckhorn Gap Trail crosses a small spring around 2.2 miles. Just beyond the spring, it leaves the road and forks to the left; the fork is marked by a carsonite sign and a large arrow in the road pointing downward (N 20' 01", W 45' 12"). The left fork is essentially a new, steep 0.25-mile shortcut, whereas the road continues gradually for 1.5 miles before the two paths reconnect. Both are excellent hikes. Those interested in the longer, mellower trail will soon cross a second spring where beech, dogwood, and Carolina silverbell are the dominant hardwoods. The road bends to the right after 0.6 mile and passes through a large and spellbindingly fragrant grove of Russian olive. The trail comes to a T intersection with F.R. 5098 after 0.75 mile, where it turns sharply to the left past an 0.25-mile-long hedge of blackberry. The road passes over a small stream after 1.2 miles. This is the same stream it crossed at the beginning; note the fascinating large stump to the left. The Buckhorn Gap Trail shortcut rejoins the main road from the left after 1.5 miles.

For the first 0.1 mile, the shortcut trail passes through a young grove that was clipped off in a storm. Afterward, the trail follows a moderate ascent beneath a canopy of Carolina silverbell and dogwood. A quarter-mile later, the Buckhorn Gap Trail ascends to F.R. 5098 and makes a sharp left. The trail leaves the gravel road and forks off to the right after 2.7 miles. You will cross two small branches in the first 20 yards, then continue for 0.2 mile to another dirt road and a major trail junction at Buckhorn Gap (N 20' 30", W 45' 05"). Entering from behind and to the right is the Black Mountain Trail. Directly across the road are two trails: to the left are the Black Mountain Trail and the Buckhorn Gap Shelter; to the right, the Buckhorn Gap Trail descends approximately 1.7 miles to the South Mills River Trail.

TWIN FALLS TRAIL (#132)

Length: 0.4 mile one way, 0.6 mile round trip
Difficulty: easy
Elevation change: 100 feet
USGS quadrant: Shining Rock
Access: The trailhead is located on the Buckhorn Gap Trail 0.7 mile north of the junction with the Avery Creek Trail (N 35° 19' 54", W 82° 45' 31"). See maps on pages 76–77.

The blue-blazed Twin Falls Trail descends to Henry Branch and crosses it three times over the first 0.1 mile. The trail is lined with partridgeberry, halberd-leaved violets, rue anemone, and occasional wild ginger. A small, cascading waterfall is located to the left after 0.25 mile. From here, the trail is lined with jack-in-the-pulpit, chickweed, and Clinton's lily. Past the cascade, you will veer to the right toward the top of the valley and the base of Twin Falls. Long, arrow-straight tulip poplar trees dominate the forest canopy in the open, wide valley. You will come to a trail junction and a large fire pit at 0.4 mile (N 20' 07", W 45' 36"). To the right beneath several large Carolina silverbells is a spur trail that reconnects with the Buckhorn Gap Trail at the horse circle after 0.1 mile; it returns to the trailhead 0.1 mile after that. To the left and right are the aptly named Twin Falls. Both falls are roughly 100 feet high and cascade with striking symmetry from separate sources to form Henry Branch. Those interested in getting a close look can follow a small footpath to the base of the left waterfall; it is ill-advised to attempt to climb any higher than this. From here, you may scramble across the land dividing the two falls to the other waterfall, where you'll find a small footpath that goes behind the cascade, then returns to the fire ring; the total loop covers approximately 0.1 mile. Near the falls are witch hazel, bee balm, dog-hobble, and some of the largest purple wake-robin trillium anywhere. From here, you can backtrack or reconnect with the Buckhorn Gap Trail via the spur trail to the right of the fire ring. Directly in front of the fire ring and across Henry Branch are the remnants of the old Buckhorn Gap Trail; do not take this trail.

AVERY CREEK TRAIL (#7)

Length: 3.2 miles one way
Difficulty: moderate if descending from Club Gap,
   moderate to strenuous if ascending
Elevation change: 1,400 feet
USGS quadrant: Shining Rock
Access: From U.S. 276 some 2.1 miles north of N.C. 280,
   turn east on F.R. 477. Drive down the dirt road for 2.3
   miles to the limited parking area on the right; you will
   pass the horse stables along the way. The trail is
   marked by a small sign (N 35° 18' 52", W 82° 44'
   56"). The other trailhead is in Club Gap (35° 20' 24",
   W 82° 46' 30"). See maps on pages 76–77.

From Club Gap, the trail descends a rocky, wide path beneath the power lines; lined with violets, the trail passes to the
right of the headwaters of Avery Creek. After 0.2 mile, it crosses
a small branch and narrows to single track. You will descend
through a large clearing after 0.8 mile, then cross a dirt road (N
20' 03", W 46' 03"). For the next 0.3 mile, the trail descends
beneath a canopy of mountain laurel with a thick underbrush
of blueberry and other heath genera. You will descend to Avery
Creek after 1.1 miles, make a sharp left, and follow a moderate-to-strenuous stretch as the trail parallels the creek. Three
tenths of a mile later, it crosses the creek. There is a spectacular
waterfall downhill to the left after 1.6 miles; a spur trail leads
to the base. A tenth of a mile later, the trail mellows out and
enters a large hemlock grove lined with dog-hobble, violets,
bloodroot, and galax. For the next 0.5 mile, it passes alongside
the creek and crosses several small tributaries lined
with sedum, rue anemone, clintonia, May apple, foamflower,
bluets, loosestrife, and aster and featuring several gorgeous

Ferns abound in Avery Creek Valley

salamanders. At 2.2 miles, you will intersect the Buckhorn Gap Trail (N 19' 22", W 45' 31"), which is marked by a wooden sign. The two trails run conjunctively for 0.1 mile before the Buckhorn Gap Trail forks off to the right, following the sign for the Upper Avery Creek Trail. The Avery Creek Trail continues ahead on a narrow footpath before crossing the creek 0.1 mile later beneath a nice grove of hemlock. After crossing two small springs, you will come to an attractive cascade to the left at 2.5 miles; it is surrounded by star chickweed, pipsissewa, and hairy buttercup. A great waterfall and swimming hole combination is to the right at 2.7 miles. Two tenths of a mile later, you will reach a trail junction. The Clawhammer Cove Trail begins straight ahead; the Avery Creek Trail makes a sharp right and crosses the creek on a sturdy footbridge. The trail begins a final ascent through a narrow thicket of rhododendron at 3.1 miles before ending at F.R. 477 some 0.1 mile later. To the right, it is 0.25 mile to the trailhead for the Buckhorn Gap Trail.

AVERY CREEK LOOP #1
Length: 4 miles round trip
Difficulty: easy
Elevation change: 500 feet
USGS quadrants: Pisgah Forest, Shining Rock

Depending upon your speed or your willingness to stop and smell the flowers, this loop can take anywhere from a couple of hours to a full day. It is a tour de force of local wildflowers. It also includes the remarkable Twin Falls.

The loop begins at the Buckhorn Gap trailhead on F.R. 477 and follows the Buckhorn Gap Trail to the Twin Falls Trail. From there, you will take the Twin Falls Trail, then loop back on to the Buckhorn Gap Trail 0.6 mile later. Once you have returned to the Twin Falls trailhead, you will backtrack 0.7 mile on the Buckhorn Gap Trail, then turn left on the Avery Creek Trail. The Avery Creek Trail and the Buckhorn Gap Trail overlap for 0.1 mile before the Avery Creek Trail forks to the left and the Buckhorn Gap Trail ascends to the right, where it is erroneously labeled "Upper Avery Creek Trail." Veer left on to the Avery Creek Trail and follow it until it ends on F.R. 477. The Buckhorn Gap trailhead is 0.25 mile to the right.

AVERY CREEK LOOP #2

Length: 9 miles round trip
Difficulty: moderate
Elevation change: 1,650 feet
USGS quadrants: Pisgah Forest, Shining Rock

This loop has all the features of the previous one, plus excellent views from Rich Mountain. It begins at the Buckhorn Gap trailhead on F.R. 477 and follows the Buckhorn Gap Trail to the Twin Falls Trail. It is highly recommended that you take the 0.6-mile Twin Falls loop before continuing north to Buckhorn Gap. At Buckhorn Gap, turn left on the Black Mountain Trail. Follow it 2.1 miles to Club Gap. At Club Gap, turn left on the Avery Creek Trail, then follow it until it ends at F.R. 477 some 0.25 mile from the starting point.

AVERY CREEK LOOP #3

Length: 12.2 miles round trip, 14.6 miles if you take one
    car and walk back to the starting point
Difficulty: strenuous
Elevation change: 2,125 feet
USGS quadrants: Pisgah Forest, Shining Rock

Technically, this isn't a loop, since it requires you to take two cars or to tramp back to the starting point; nonetheless, it is well worth the effort. The trail essentially circumnavigates the entire Avery Creek Valley. The "loop" begins on the Black Mountain Trail off U.S. 276 and follows it for its entirety to Club Gap. At Club Gap, continue straight across on to the Buckwheat Knob Trail. The Buckwheat Knob Trail will take you to Bennett Gap, and the Bennett Gap Trail will return you to

F.R. 477. To the right, it is 1.4 miles to U.S. 276, then an additional 1 mile to the left back to the starting point.

Note: There is an option for this loop that doesn't require a second car. You may omit the first 2.7 miles of the Black Mountain Trail by beginning on the Pressley Cove Trail, which is located across the road from the end of the Bennett Gap Trail. The Pressley Cove Trail isn't included in this book, however, because it is so steep. If you choose this option, follow the Pressley Cove Trail for 1.1 miles, then turn right on the dirt road. After 0.2 mile, you'll reach Pressley Gap. Turn left on the Black Mountain Trail and proceed from there. This loop is 10.8 miles round trip.

AVERY CREEK LOOP #4
Length: 4.1 miles round trip
Difficulty: strenuous
Elevation change: 1,100 feet
USGS quadrants: Pisgah Forest, Shining Rock

This short but strenuous hike will take you from a small cove to some incredible overlooks. Begin the Perry Cove Trail off F.R. 477. When the trail ends at Saddle Gap, it is highly recommended that you hike 0.25 mile to the right on the Bennett Gap Trail, where there are two incredible overlooks—one to the west and one to the east. Once you have enjoyed both overlooks, turn around and follow the Bennett Gap Trail 1.9 miles back down to F.R. 477. The Perry Cove trailhead is 0.6 mile to the left.

COURTHOUSE CREEK AREA

Between Tanasee Ridge to the west and Shuck Ridge to the east lie the headwaters of the French Broad River. Courthouse Creek is both the northernmost and the highest of those headwaters, beginning over a mile high near the Devil's Courthouse. This massive rock outcropping derives its name from an old Cherokee legend. In Cherokee mythology, a devilishly evil spirit named Judaculla resided in a cave, where he presided over his courtroom.

DEVIL'S COURTHOUSE TRAIL

Length: 0.4 mile one way
Difficulty: moderate to strenuous
Elevation change: 300 feet
USGS quadrant: Sam Knob
Access: The trail is located on the Blue Ridge Parkway at
the large Devil's Courthouse Parking Area near
Milepost 422.4; the parking area is 1 mile east of
N.C. 215 (N 35° 18' 19", W 82° 53' 56").

This short but strenuous hike offers one of the most commanding views anywhere in the national forest. From the rock's edge, you can see into Georgia, Tennessee, and South Carolina.

For the first 100 yards, the trail is paved and parallels the parkway. Then it forks to the right and begins a strenuous climb through a spruce/fir forest. After 0.3 mile, it bends to the right and a spur trail forks off to the left; the 0.1-mile spur trail connects to the Mountains-to-Sea Trail (N 18' 16", W 53' 42"). A tenth of a mile later, the trail ends at the rock wall of an observation deck that offers an astonishing panorama. Beginning to the far left, you will see Black Mountain at 83° and 9.3 miles, Looking Glass Rock at 94° and 5.7 miles, Cedar Rock at 125° and 6.2 miles, Three Forks Mountain at 152° and 6.8 miles, Pinnacle Mountain in South Carolina at 159° and 20.5 miles, Musterground Mountain near Lake Jocassee in South Carolina at 194° and 20.6 miles, Bald Knob at 206° and 4.3 miles, Toxaway Mountain behind Lake Toxaway at 207° and 12.8 miles, Rabun Bald in Georgia at 228° and 32.6 miles, Double Knob at 229° and 13.7 miles, Tanasee Bald at 242° and 1.4 miles, Bear Knob at 242° and 11.9 miles, Sheep Knob at 265° and 19.9 miles, Mount Hardy at 278° and 1.8 miles, Clingmans Dome at 302°

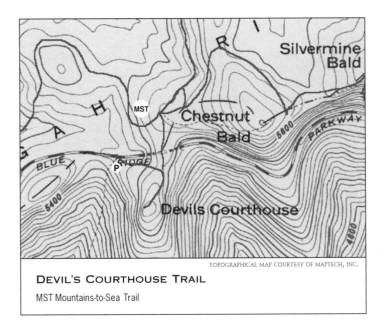

TOPOGRAPHICAL MAP COURTESY OF MAPTECH, INC.

DEVIL'S COURTHOUSE TRAIL

MST Mountains-to-Sea Trail

and 38.4 miles, Balsam Knob at 314° and 6.9 miles, Plot Balsam at 322° and 16.4 miles, Green Knob at 327° and 2.5 miles, Mount Guyot in Tennessee at 328° and 43.4 miles, Lickstone Bald at 337° and 9.5 miles, High Top at 353° and 5.8 miles, Ratcliff Mountain at 356° and 12.8 miles, Max Patch at 358° and 34.3 miles, Little Sam Knob at 2° and 1.2 miles, and Sam Knob at 6° and 1.8 miles.

Length: 2.1 miles one way
Difficulty: easy to moderate, with a short strenuous section
    at the end
Elevation change: 360 feet
USGS quadrant: Sam Knob
Access: From N.C. 215 some 10.6 miles north of U.S. 64
    or 7.5 miles south of the Blue Ridge Parkway, turn on
    to F.R. 140, a dirt road. You will drive over a bridge at
    3.1 miles; there is a parking area to the right. The trail
    begins to the left (N 35° 16' 26", W 82° 53' 32").

The blue-blazed trail—lined with dog-hobble, wood betony, white and purple violets, galax, and bluets beneath a canopy of rhododendron, Eastern hemlock, and red oak—begins along the right side of Courthouse Creek. After 0.25 mile, the creek drops considerably in elevation, so that the trail is now 100 feet above it. The Courthouse Falls Trail switches down to the left at 0.3 mile (N 16' 16", W 53' 42"). There is a good campsite at 0.5 mile (N 16' 19", W 53' 52"). A hundred yards later, the trail crosses Mill Station Creek on a footbridge. It rounds a corner to the right at 0.8 mile, then heads south for 0.25 mile along a large, open clearing on the mountainside; you'll see lots of Carolina silverbells, dogwood, wild oats, bloodroot, Solomon's-seal, columbine, staghorn sumac, wild hydrangea, and foamflower along the way. If you turn around and look directly north, you'll see a large rock outcropping 2.4 miles in the distance; this is the Devil's Courthouse, revered by the Cherokees as the site where the devil Judaculla held court. From where you are standing, water to the north flows into Courthouse Creek, while water to the south flows into Summey Cove

Creek; the two creeks merge to the east and form the North Fork of the French Broad River. You will reach a potentially confusing trail junction at 1.3 miles (N 15' 52", W 53' 47"). The Summey Cove Trail, marked by a blue blaze, turns sharply to the left; the footpath straight ahead goes nowhere. Shortly thereafter, you will cross the small Summey Cove Creek. A hundred yards later, the trail becomes rather steep. It crosses a dirt road at 1.5 miles (N 15' 47", W 53' 56"). You will climb some wooden steps through lots of

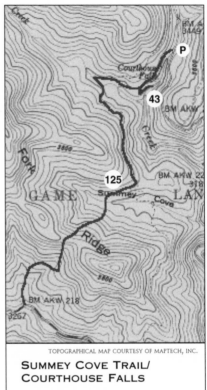

TOPOGRAPHICAL MAP COURTESY OF MAPTECH, INC.

**SUMMEY COVE TRAIL/
COURTHOUSE FALLS**

43 Courthouse Falls Trail
125 Summey Cove Trail

Pierus and flame azalea and begin a moderate-to-strenuous ascent of the ridge. The trail crests the ridge beneath a thicket of mountain laurel at 1.7 miles (N 15' 42", W 54' 3"). From the crest, you will descend steeply for 0.1 mile, after which the trail becomes more moderate. At 2.1 miles, the trail ends at N.C. 215 just before a bridge (N 15' 27", W 54' 17").

Length: 0.2 mile round trip
Difficulty: Moderate, but short
Elevation change: 80 feet
USGS quadrant: Sam Knob
Access: Follow the directions for the Summey Cove Trail. Three tenths of a mile down the Summey Cove Trail, the Courthouse Falls Trail drops off to the left (N 16' 16", W 53' 42"). See map on page 97.

The orange-blazed trail descends a mere 0.1 mile to the spectacular Courthouse Falls (N 16' 17", W 53' 39"). Located in the middle of a horseshoe-shaped rock wall lined with ferns and bluets, the falls are nearly 50 feet high. They plunge into a stunning emerald swimming pool. Beneath the walls are jack-in-the-pulpit, sweet shrub, wood anemone, and yellow birch. There are no places to camp at the falls, but one could spend hours here rock-hopping.

OTHER TRAILS IN THE PISGAH RANGER DISTRICT

PINK BEDS LOOP TRAIL (#106)
Length: 3.3 miles (previously 5 miles)
Difficulty: easy
Elevation change: 100 feet
USGS quadrangles: Shining Rock, Pisgah Forest
Access: From U.S. 276 some 11.6 miles north of N.C.
    280 in Brevard and 3.7 miles south of the Blue Ridge
    Parkway, turn into the Pink Beds Parking Area. The
    trail begins on an old dirt road behind a gate (N 35°
    21' 11", 82° 46' 44"). See map on page 100.

Previously, this was a 5-mile loop trail. However, in the past few years, some remarkably industrious beavers have erected a series of dams that effectively flooded a 0.25-mile section of the trail. You can still hike both ends of the trail up to the flood point and then backtrack, or you can use the Mountains-to-Sea Trail Alternate for a 3.3-mile loop instead. Either way, you will enjoy a splendid, easy stroll through a unique mountain ecosystem crisscrossed by the headwaters of the South Fork of the Mills River.

The orange-blazed trail descends on the gravel roadbed,

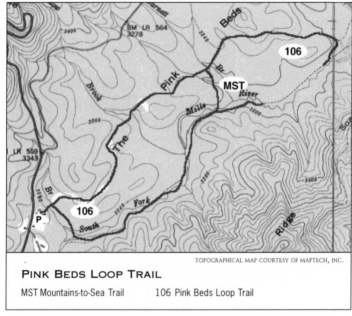

TOPOGRAPHICAL MAP COURTESY OF MAPTECH, INC.

PINK BEDS LOOP TRAIL

MST Mountains-to-Sea Trail   106 Pink Beds Loop Trail

crosses Pigeon Branch, and comes to a fork after 0.1 mile, where it veers off to the right (N 21' 13", W 46' 39"). The wide, serpentine trail winds alongside the headwaters of the South Fork of the Mills River through a dense cover of mountain laurel, rhododendron, white pine, Carolina silverbell, hemlock, oak, dog-hobble, Southern lady fern, cinnamon fern, galax, partridge-berry, club moss, hawthorn, ground cedar, pale jewelweed, witch hazel, bluets, wood and rue anemone, trout lily, various violets and trilliums, and buttercups. A well-constructed network of wooden footbridges traverses the South Fork of the Mills River and its various tributaries at 0.2 mile, again 75 yards later, at 0.5 mile, at 0.8 mile, at 1.1 miles, at 1.2 miles, at 1.6 miles, and again at 2.5 miles. The Mountains-to-Sea Trail Alternate (MST-A) intersects the Pink Beds Loop Trail at 1.6 miles (N 21' 38", W 45' 40"). Previously, the Pink Beds Loop Trail followed the MST-A to the right, then branched off to the left after 50 yards. You still can take the old trail for about 0.3 mile before it becomes submerged. Unless you want to follow the old trail to the water, turn left on the MST-A. You will come to a trail intersection and a large campsite at 1.9 miles (N 21' 49", W 45' 47"). To the left, the Pink Beds Loop Trail returns to the parking lot; straight ahead, the MST-A continues 0.6 mile to F.R. 1206; to the right, the Pink Beds Loop Trail heads toward another section of the beaver dam and the Gagging Station Trail. (If you decide to follow the loop trail to the right, you will ascend a small hill, then descend into a sublime hardwood forest blanketed with acres of Southern lady fern. After 1 mile in this direction, you will reach a trail junction and three carsonite signs [N 21' 54", W 45' 0"]. The Gagging Station Trail breaks off to the left and goes 0.9 mile to F.R. 476; the Pink Beds Loop Trail turns right and passes a nice creek-side campsite on the left after 20 yards. You will pass one section of the beaver dam to the left at 1.3 mile. A hundred yards later, the trail peters out into the water.) From the campsite at the 1.9-mile mark, the Pink Beds Loop Trail resumes to the left. It leaves the laurel slick at 2.4 miles and enters a large meadow on an old road. The trail follows the road for 0.9 mile back to the fork mentioned in the first sentence. From here, the parking lot is 0.1 mile straight ahead.

MOUNT PISGAH TRAIL (#92)

Length: 1.3 miles one way
Difficulty: moderate
Elevation change: 750 feet
USGS quadrangles: Cruso, Dunsmore Mountain
Access: From Milepost 407.6 on the Blue Ridge Parkway,
    turn south into the parking area and drive to the
    trailhead, located at the far eastern end of the parking
    lot (N 35° 25' 5", W 82° 44' 52"). A large wooden sign
    here notes the trailhead and the biblical passage from
    which the mountain derives its name.

The trail follows an easy grade on a wide, rocky path through mountain laurel, yellow birch, rhododendron (*maximum, calendulaceum*, and *viscosum*), houstonia, bluets, moosewood, false Solomon's-seal, fly poison, love vine, columbine, fire pink, viburnum, yarrow, blueberry, thimbleberry, Dutchman's-pipe, and lady, Christmas, maidenhair, and cinnamon ferns. After 0.5 mile, the grade becomes moderate; you will enjoy nice views to the north. Shortly thereafter, the trail narrows and the grade becomes moderate to strenuous. The trail reaches the summit (5,721 feet, N 25' 32", W 45' 24") at 1.3 miles, where you'll find a large, wooden observation deck and a television tower surrounded by bush honeysuckle, mountain laurel, and fire cherry. Beginning to the north, you'll see Camp Creek Bald at 7° and 41.3 miles, Newfound Mountain at 8° and 10.6 miles, Highrock Ridge at 11° and 31.2 miles, Frozen Knob at 20° and 33.4 miles (both Highrock Ridge and Frozen Knob are in the Walnut Mountains), Big Bald at 25° and 41.8 miles, Celo Knob at 48° and 41.1 miles, Mount Mitchell at 54° and 36.3 miles, the Biltmore House at 60° and 14 miles, Greybeard

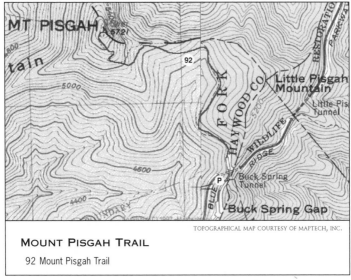

TOPOGRAPHICAL MAP COURTESY OF MAPTECH, INC.

MOUNT PISGAH TRAIL

92 Mount Pisgah Trail

Mountain at 60° and 31.5 miles, High Windy at 71° and 25.6 miles, Little Pisgah Mountain at 82° and 24.4 miles, Bank Mountain at 93° and 19.9 miles, Little Bald Mountain at 158° and 1.4 miles, Black Mountain at 173° and 6.9 miles, Cedar Rock at 196° and 11.9 miles, Pilot Mountain at 215° and 12.2 miles, Fork River Bald at 221° and 9.6 miles, Black Balsam Knob at 229° and 9.5 miles, Shining Rock at 240° and 7.1 miles, Balsam Knob at 257° and 13.8 miles, Cold Mountain at 263° and 5.7 miles, Mount Le Conte (TN) at 296° and 41.3 miles, Grassy Bald at 273° and 16.7 miles, Lickstone Bald at 274° and 12.1 miles, Clingmans Dome at 287° and 42.8 miles, Ratcliff Mountain at 298° and 10.4 miles, Mount Guyot at 309° and 34.1 miles, Mount Sterling at 317° and 28 miles, Sandymush Bald at 342° and 18.9 miles, and Thompson Knob at 354° and 6.6 miles.

Note: The Pilot Cove/Slate Rock Creek Trail begins in Pilot Cove, crosses Slate Rock Ridge, and ends in Slate Rock Creek Cove. However, in order to create two enjoyable loop trails, this single trail is described as two distinct trails, one beginning in Pilot Cove and the other at Slate Rock Creek.

PILOT COVE TRAIL (#102)

Length: 1.3 miles
Difficulty: easy for the first mile, moderate to strenuous for the last 0.3 mile
Elevation change: 840 feet
USGS quadrant: Dunsmore Mountain
Access: The trailhead is on F.R. 1206. If you are approaching from the west, turn off U.S. 276 on to F.R. 1206 some 3.3 miles south of the parkway or 12 miles north of N.C. 280, then drive 5.3 miles east to the trailhead, located on the left. If you are coming from the east, turn off N.C. 191 on to North Mills River Road (S.R. 1345). After 5.7 miles, the pavement ends and F.R. 1206 begins. The trailhead is on the right after 7.1 miles (N 35° 22' 59", W 82° 42' 54").

The trail begins on an easy slope to the right of Pilot Cove Creek through lots of rhododendron, dog-hobble, mountain laurel, galax, trillium, May apple, umbrella-leaf, violets, purple-crested dwarf iris, trout lily, foamflower, Indian cucumber, fly poison, sweet shrub, and mixed hardwoods. After 0.1 mile, the southern terminus of the Pilot Cove Loop Trail descends from the right. The main trail continues straight ahead and crosses the creek on a wooden footbridge 0.1 mile later. Soon after the footbridge, the trail seems to disappear into a bog; recent beaver

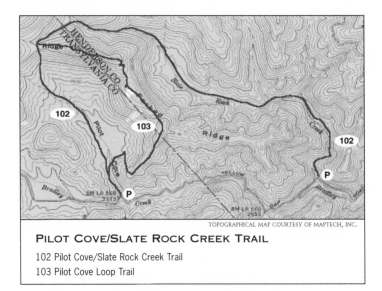

TOPOGRAPHICAL MAP COURTESY OF MAPTECH, INC.

PILOT COVE/SLATE ROCK CREEK TRAIL

102 Pilot Cove/Slate Rock Creek Trail
103 Pilot Cove Loop Trail

activity has flooded a short section of the trail around the 0.3-mile mark. It is possible to bypass the flooded terrain by bush-whacking to the left for about 30 yards, then looping back to the right to reconnect with the original trail. There is a small campsite to the right at 0.4 mile. Almost 0.5 mile later, the ascent becomes moderate to strenuous. The trail veers to the right away from the creek bed, passes a series of old wooden posts, and climbs Slate Rock Ridge. You will reach the ridge crest at 1.3 miles, where the Pilot Cove Loop Trail begins to the right (N 23' 53", W 43' 29"). Straight ahead, the Pilot Cove/Slate Rock Creek Trail descends toward Slate Rock Creek.

The Civilian Conservation Corps

That we are presently able to access and enjoy Pisgah National Forest is largely due to the efforts of the thousands of Civilian Conservation Corps (CCC) workers who were assigned to western North Carolina between 1933 and 1941. Established on the fifth day of Franklin Delano Roosevelt's presidency, the CCC was one of the most successful of the New Deal programs that allowed the United States to lift itself out of the Great Depression.

When the program began, 27 percent of North Carolinians were unemployed. The mountain region was especially hard hit. Nationwide, over 5 million young people were out of work, homeless, and largely out of hope. The CCC was initially open to single men between the ages of 18 and 25. The volunteers had to be unemployed. They had to commit to a six-month stay and be willing to work for $30 per month, $22 of which was sent home to their needy families.

According to Roosevelt, the CCC's mission was "simple work, not interfering with normal employment, and confining itself to forestry, the prevention of soil erosion, flood control, and similar projects." Equally important were the less tangible goals of increasing the moral and spiritual fiber of young Americans who were disheartened and downtrodden by economic hardship.

The CCC was a cooperative effort among government agencies. The Department of Labor recruited enrollees; the Department of the Army housed, fed, vaccinated, and conditioned them; and the Department of Agriculture and the Department of the Interior put them to work.

The program was well received from the outset. Some 250,000 young men, 25,000 war veterans, and 25,000 experienced woodsmen were at work in 1,468 CCC camps nationwide within three months.

North Carolina embraced the CCC and enjoyed its benefits. Over 75,000 North Carolinians participated. At the height of the program, there were CCC camps in 60 of the state's 100 counties. A 1939 Associated Press story estimated that the families of North Carolina CCC employees had received over $14 million for their enrollees' work. Near Pisgah Forest, camps were located at Barnardsville, Mars Hill, Hot Springs, Asheville, Old Fort, Marion, Bakersville, Sunburst, Balsam Grove, Arden, the North Mills River, Brevard, John's Rock, and Mount Mitchell. Eight additional camps were located in Great Smoky Mountains National Park.

Life in a CCC camp was regimented and productive. A typical camp consisted of 200 men commanded by an army captain. Their work was supervised by a Forest Service foreman and local woodsmen. From reveille until sundown, the workers built roads and trails, fought fires, planted trees, cleared brush, constructed shelters, manned fire towers, and carried out other conservation activities. In the evening, classes were available for illiterate or undereducated CCC workers. They worked five and a half days per week. On weekends, they were able to venture into local communities and mingle with the natives. Many workers assigned to western North Carolina were from large cities in the Northeast. Their infusion into towns such as Bryson City, Brevard, Hot Springs, and Franklin was immediately felt. The cultural exchange was a bonus for both the natives and the workers.

The CCC ended when the economic and military demands of World War II strengthened the United States economy and required the services of all available young men. But the program's legacy is omnipresent in Pisgah Forest even today—in the trails, the campsites, the trees, the soil, the streams, and the region's history.

PILOT COVE LOOP TRAIL (#103)

Length: 2.1 miles one way
Difficulty: moderate
Elevation change: 750 feet
USGS quadrant: Dunsmore Mountain
Access: The northern trailhead is located in a saddle on
    Slate Rock Ridge (N 35° 23' 53", W 82° 43' 29"). The
    southern trailhead is on Pilot Cove/Slate Rock Creek
    Trail some 0.1 mile from F.R. 1206 (N 35° 23' 7", W
    82° 42' 59"). See map on page 105.

From the northern trailhead on Slate Rock Ridge, you will walk eastward along the ridge top through blueberry, mountain laurel, false downy foxglove, and white snakeroot. After 0.25 mile, the trail crests the ridge. Twenty yards later, a small spur trail breaks off to the right; the spur trail offers an excellent view of Cedar Rock at 205° and 10.7 miles. Shortly thereafter, the main trail begins a short moderate-to-strenuous descent of a series of switchbacks to a saddle before ascending back up the ridge. You will come to a fantastic rock exposure at 0.9 miles, where there are stands of weathered table mountain pine and water-carved pools in the rock; you will see the cliffs of Pilot Rock at 275°, Beech Knob at 267° and 3.8 miles, Green Knob at 246° and 5.5 miles, Fork River Bald at 241° and 9.9 miles, Pilot Mountain at 230° and 12 miles, Rich Mountain at 225° and 4.8 miles, and Funneltop Mountain directly across to the south. Eastern Timber Rattlesnakes have been known to nest in this area in the past. Although the timber rattler is poisonous, its bite is rarely fatal. More importantly, it is rarely aggressive and will not bite humans unless seriously molested or provoked. Please take care when approaching this overlook. If you make noise on the approach, you will probably never see a snake. From the overlook, the trail descends gradually for 0.5 mile, then switches down sharply to the right and follows a moderate descent for 0.4 mile. From there, it switches down to the right again, follows a moderate descent for almost 0.2 mile, switches back sharply to the left, and passes above Pilot Cove Creek for 0.1 mile before ending at the junction with Pilot Cove/Slate Rock Creek Trail (N 23' 7", W 42' 59").

SLATE ROCK CREEK TRAIL (#102)

Length: 3 miles one way
Difficulty: moderate for the first 2.5 miles, strenuous
    thereafter
Elevation change: 1,000 feet
USGS quadrant: Dunsmore Mountain
Access: The trailhead is on F.R. 1206. If you are
    approaching from the west, turn off U.S. 276 on to
    F.R. 1206 some 3.3 miles south of the parkway or 12
    miles north of N.C. 280; drive 7.1 miles east to the
    trailhead, on the left. If you are coming from the east,
    turn off N.C. 191 on to North Mills River Road (S.R.
    1345). After 5.7 miles, the pavement ends and F.R.
    1206 begins. The trailhead is on the right 5.5 miles
    down the road (N 35° 23' 6", W 82° 41' 31"). See
    map on page 105.

The blue-blazed trail begins to the right of Slate Rock Creek on an easy slope through lots of hawthorn, sycamore, witch hazel, maidenhair fern, Christmas fern, mountain laurel, dog-hobble, purple-crested dwarf iris, spring beauty, bloodroot, trout lily, white erect trillium, jack-in-the-pulpit, Vacey's trillium, and great lobelia. There is a good swimming hole at 0.2 mile. A tenth of a mile later, you will cross a small branch from the right. The trail descends to an old roadbed after 0.5 mile and veers to the right. You will cross a creek a 0.8 mile and again 0.2 mile later. At 1.3 miles, there is an excellent campsite where the creek splits, creating a small island beneath a canopy of large hemlock and yellow birch (N 23' 33", W 42' 2"). Almost 0.5 mile later, the creek valley opens into a spacious and flat meadow blanketed with acres of lady and cinnamon ferns beneath locust, white oak, red maple, yellow birch, and dogwood. There is a tricky stream crossing at 2.2 miles. Descending from the right is an attractive, small waterfall; the trail cuts across the narrow and often slippery rocks beneath the falls. Four tenths of a mile later, the trail comes to a confusing intersection. Here, you will pass a tulip poplar that has several blue blazes painted on it. An old trail continues straight ahead; the Slate Rock Creek Trail crosses the stream to the left, then veers to the right, following the blue blaze on a yellow birch (N 24' 1", W 43' 12"). From here, you will pass through a grove of young hemlock on a path lined with galax, meadow rue, and lady's-slipper. You will then begin a moderate-to-strenuous ascent, crossing a small footbridge 0.1 mile later. After 3 miles, you will crest a ridge and reach a junction with the Pilot Cove Loop Trail to the left. Straight ahead, the Pilot Cove/Slate Rock Creek Trail descends into Pilot Cove (N 23' 53", W 43' 29").

GRANDFATHER

RANGER

DISTRICT

LINVILLE GORGE WILDERNESS AREA

The Linville Gorge Wilderness Area encompasses one of the largest and most remote river gorges in the eastern United States. The Linville River cuts a deep, rocky channel through the gorge as it descends 2,000 feet in 17 miles. The highest point is Gingercake Mountain at 4,120 feet; the lowest point is 1,250 feet at the southern end of the river. On average, the gorge is 1.5 miles wide and 1,300 feet deep, though in some places it is more than 2 miles wide and 1,750 feet deep. Both sides of the gorge are lined with miles of jagged cliffs, often several hundred vertical feet high, which make this a mecca for rock climbers.

The roughness of the terrain has always made logging difficult here. For this reason, some of the most remote coves still contain pockets of virgin timber. The gorge is home to several species of rare or endangered plants. Eastern and Carolina hemlock take on mythic proportions in Linville Gorge—some of them are large enough to walk through! There are literally dozens of species of deciduous trees and too many flowering plants to list. From the first thaw to the end of fall, there is always something in bloom here. The Linville River is also prized among trout fishermen.

Linville Gorge was named after explorer William Linville and his son, John, who were killed in the gorge by Cherokees in 1766. The Cherokees refer to the river as Eeseeoh, or "River of Many Cliffs."

The gorge was designated a Wilderness Area in 1951. In 1964, it became one of the original components of the National Wilderness System. Twenty years later, when the North Carolina Wilderness Act was signed, the original 7,575-acre plot was expanded to its current 10,975 acres.

There are well over 20 trails covering nearly 50 miles in Linville Gorge. All but two—the Rock Jock Trail and a section of the Mountains-to-Sea Trail—are covered in detail in this chapter. The four trails at Linville Falls are not connected with the other trails; in fact, they belong to the Blue Ridge Parkway. The Linville Gorge Trail runs parallel to the river on its western bank for almost 12 miles and is accessible via numerous trails that descend from Kistler Memorial Highway to the west. The trails on the eastern side are not as interconnected. Instead, they focus on the magnificent overlooks and rock exposures of the ridge tops. Four trails—Brushy Ridge, Devil's Hole, Spence Ridge, and Cambric Branch—descend from the eastern rim to the river. Spence Ridge is usually the only trail that is used to cross the river, and even it isn't a sure thing. The Jonas Ridge Trail, the Hawksbill Trail, the Table Rock Summit Trail, and the Shortoff Mountain Trail all offer astounding vistas of the gorge and the mountains beyond.

Because the gorge is a protected Wilderness Area, there is

little trail maintenance or marking. It is notorious for getting people lost. Dozens of experienced hikers have gotten lost here. In fact, one of the authors of this guide once spent an unprepared December night here during grade school. Because the trails are rough, remote, and unblazed, solid back-country skills are a must. In addition, please respect the no-trace policy of the Forest Service and keep the wild in the wilderness.

LINVILLE FALLS TRAILS

Technically speaking, these trails are not part of Pisgah National Forest; instead, they are part of a 440-acre plot that belongs to the National Park Service. Nonetheless, it would be silly to exclude these four excellent, short day hikes because of a technicality. A couple of these trails provide multiple vantage points of the famous Linville Falls, while the others are just simple, great hikes. All of them are heavily visited, however, so don't expect much solitude, and please don't leave the main trail. It is not possible to connect any of these four trails with the other trails in Linville Gorge.

There are two ways to access these trails. One parking lot is located on Kistler Memorial Highway (Old N.C. 105). From N.C. 183, turn south on to the dirt road, following the signs for Linville Gorge. The first parking area you will come to is the large Linville Falls Parking Area (N 35° 56' 59", W 81° 51' 1"). The other parking lot is located off the Blue Ridge Parkway.

Near Milepost 316.4, turn south on to the Linville Falls Recreation Area Access Road. Follow it until it ends at the visitor center (35° 57' 17", W 81° 55' 40"). The four trails may be combined for a round trip of 5 miles from the dirt parking lot or 4.2 miles from the parkway parking lot.

LINVILLE FALLS TRAIL
Length: 1.8 miles or 2 miles round trip
Difficulty: easy to moderate
Elevation change: 150 feet
USGS quadrant: Linville Falls

This trail encompasses four distinct overlooks that branch off one main trial. From the dirt parking lot on Kistler Memorial Highway, the trail begins a moderate descent of a well-worn old road lined with several species of rhododendron, hemlock, umbrella magnolia, mountain laurel, sassafras, fire pink, trout lily, violets, dogwood, trillium, thalictrum, and cohosh. You will come to a junction marked by a wooden sign at 0.3 mile (N 56' 58", W 55' 45"). The Linville Falls Trail veers off to the right; a wide dirt road wraps around to the left and

Linville Falls Trail

continues 0.4 mile to the paved parking lot at Linville Falls Recreation Area, where you can access the Plunge Basin Overlook Trail, the Linville Gorge Trail, and the Duggers Creek Loop Trail. A second trail intersection is located on the right after another 30 yards. The trail to the Upper Falls Overlook descends to the left; the trails to Chimney Overlook and Erwin's View fork off to the right. The trail to the Upper Falls Overlook descends for 0.1

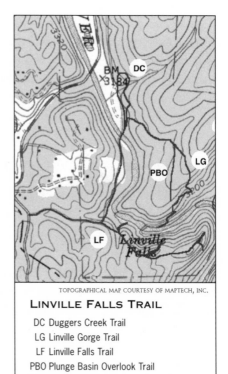

TOPOGRAPHICAL MAP COURTESY OF MAPTECH, INC.

LINVILLE FALLS TRAIL

DC Duggers Creek Trail
LG Linville Gorge Trail
LF Linville Falls Trail
PBO Plunge Basin Overlook Trail

mile to a rock wall at the top of Linville Falls; despite the inviting pool, it goes without saying that swimming here is a *really* dumb idea. From the second trail intersection, you will follow an easy-to-moderate ascent through mixed hardwoods. After 0.25 mile, you will come to a covered picnic table and a trail junction. The trail to Chimney View Overlook descends to the left; the trail to Erwin's View continues straight ahead. The trail to Chimney View Overlook makes an easy descent alongside a wooden guardrail and offers yet another outstanding vantage point overlooking Linville Falls. If you turn right at the covered picnic table, it is about 200 before the trail ends at a small rock wall that offers excellent views to the south of the gorge. Immediately before the wall, a trail breaks off to the left to Erwin's View. From Erwin's View, you can enjoy a good view of Humpback Mountain at 257° and 2.4 miles, Doe Hill Mountain at 303° and 3.2 miles, and Buck Hill at 319° and 11.3 miles.

PLUNGE BASIN OVERLOOK TRAIL

Length: 0.5 mile one way
Difficulty: easy to moderate
Elevation change: 100 feet
USGS quadrant: Linville Falls
Access: See map on page 117.

The Plunge Basin Overlook Trail and the Linville Gorge Trail begin to the right of the visitor center. For 0.3 mile, the two trails run conjunctively beneath an acidic forest of Eastern hemlock and rhododendron. The Linville Gorge Trail forks off to the left at 0.3 mile; the Plunge Basin Overlook Trail continues straight ahead. Continuing on the Plunge Basin Overlook Trail, you will pass beneath a high, dense tunnel of mountain laurel. Two tenths of a mile later, the trail ends at Plunge Basin Overlook. The aptly named overlook peers out from the northern wall of the gorge at the nearly lake-sized plunge basin and the magnificent waterfall.

LINVILLE GORGE TRAIL (BLUE RIDGE PARKWAY)
Length: 0.7 mile one way
Difficulty: moderate to strenuous
Elevation change: 300 feet
USGS quadrant: Linville Falls
Access: See map on page 117.

The Plunge Basin Overlook Trail and the Linville Gorge Trail begin to the right of the visitor center. For 0.3 mile, the two trails run conjunctively beneath an acidic forest of Eastern hemlock and rhododendron. The Linville Gorge Trail forks off to the left at 0.3 mile; the Plunge Basin Overlook Trail continues straight ahead. The Linville Gorge Trail quickly narrows and becomes rocky and difficult to negotiate. It follows a moderate-to-strenuous descent for 0.2 mile, then switches back sharply to the right at the base of a huge rock wall. Two tenths of a mile later, you will reach the shore of the Plunge Basin—a magnificent, immense pool at the base of Linville Falls. Directly overhead is the Plunge Basin Overlook; directly across the river is the Upper Falls Overlook; and farther to the left is the Chimney Overlook.

DUGGERS CREEK LOOP
Length: 0.4 mile round trip
Difficulty: easy
Elevation change: 75 feet
USGS quadrant: Linville Falls
Access: See map on page 117.

This is an excellent, short, meditative loop. The narrow trail begins beneath enormous hemlock, rhododendron, mountain laurel, sassafras, and umbrella magnolia. After 0.1 mile, it comes to a T intersection on an old roadbed. To the right, it is 0.1 mile to a junction with the Plunge Basin Overlook Trail; the loop trail continues to the left. Forty yards later, the trail makes a sharp right away from the parking area, marked by orange tape on two rhododendrons. It crosses Duggers Creek on a wooden footbridge at 0.2 mile; the small, captivating waterfall to your right creates its own miniature gorge as it carves a deep channel into the rocky cove. You will ascend a rock staircase before veering to the left. From there, the trail gradually bends back to the south; along the way is posted a series of contemplative naturalist quotations. The trail veers sharply to the left, rock-hops across Duggers Creek, and turns to asphalt as it heads back to the trailhead.

West Rim Trails

The magnificent trails on the West Rim of Linville Gorge range from simple ridge walks and riverside hikes to strenuous, remote scrambles down rocky, lush coves. All the trails begin off Kistler Memorial Highway, a dirt road otherwise known as Old N.C. 105. To reach Kistler Memorial Highway, turn south off N.C. 183 some 0.7 mile east of U.S. 221 and 4.4 miles west of N.C. 181 at a sharp bend in the road marked by a wooden Forest Service sign.

You will come to the Linville Falls Parking Area at 0.1 mile. There is parking for Pine Gap Trail at 0.8 mile, for Bynum Bluff Trail at 1.5 miles, for Cabin Trail at 1.9 miles, for Babel Tower Trail at 2.7 miles, for Sandy Flats Trail at 3.8 miles. The road to Wiseman's View forks off to the left 0.1 mile later. There is parking for Conley Cove Trail at 5.4 miles and for Pinch-In Trail at 8.5 miles.

LINVILLE GORGE TRAIL (#231)

Length: 11.2 miles
Difficulty: moderately steep, difficult to negotiate
Elevation change: 1,600 feet
USGS quadrants: Linville Falls, Ashford
Access: There is no roadside access to this trail. You must use one of the seven trails off Kistler Memorial Highway from the west or either the Devil's Hole Trail or the Spence Ridge Gap Trail from the east. See maps on pages 122–123.

The trail begins at the intersection of the Pine Gap Trail and the Bynum Bluff Trail. After 50 yards, you will reach a small spur trail leading to the campsite on the Bynum Bluff Trail. The trail continues an easy decent through mountain laurel and mixed hardwoods. There is a spectacular small overlook at 0.4 mile that offers a clear view to the northeast of the cliffs of Brushy Ridge. A tenth of a mile later, the trail switches back several times, then passes alongside a rock ledge utterly dripping with moss. A spur trail descends to a riverside campsite on the left at 0.7 mile, just downstream from where the river shelf drops 10 feet, creating a waterfall and a massive swimming hole. The trail ascends steeply, then wraps around a ridge line to the right at 1.2 miles and intersects the Cabin Trail (N 55' 44", W 55' 8"). Note that the Cabin Trail is easily missed; if you are trying to find it, you should look for "C-A-B-I-N" carved into a 12-inch red maple and a rectangular rock with two arrows scratched into it. From here, you will continue an easy

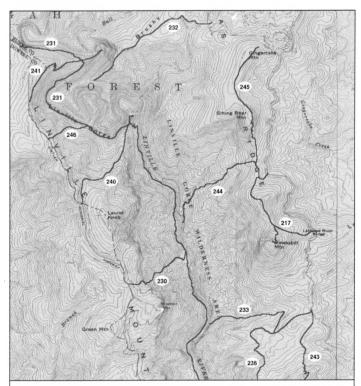

LINVILLE GORGE TRAILS

CB Cambric Branch Trail	217 Hawksbill Trail
228 Pinch-In Trail	229 Conley Cove Trail
230 Sandy Flats Trail	231 Linville Gorge Trail
232 Brushy Ridge Trail	233 Spence Ridge Trail
235 Shortoff Mountain Trail	236 Little Table Rock Trail
240 Babel Tower Trail	241 Bynum Bluff Trail
242 Table Rock Summit Trail	243 Table Rock Gap Trail
244 Devil's HoleTrail	245 Jonas Ridge Trail
246 Cabin Trail	

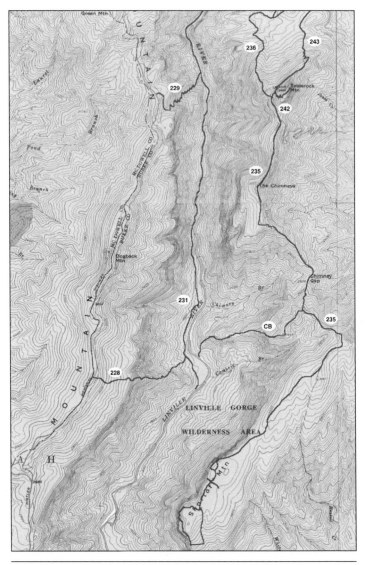

View of Linville Gorge

descent along the ridge contour into a narrow cove high above the river. You will enter an old-growth hemlock grove at 1.6 miles, where the trail becomes rather tricky. There is a fair-sized branch to the left, marked by a piece of red tape on a rhododendron; the trail crosses the branch and follows the *orange* tape on the other side, *not* the red tape to your left. Once you find the proper trail, you will begin a moderate-to-strenuous ascent out of the cove, then crest a ridge at 2 miles, where the Babel Tower Trail ascends to the right and left (N 55' 45", W 54' 40"). From the saddle, it is an easy-to-moderate descent on a narrow path lined with rhododendron, hemlock, mountain laurel, goldenrod, and mountain gentian. After 0.1 mile, the trail switches down to the left for 75 yards, then switches back to the right. There is another switchback 100 yards later; straight ahead is an awesome vista of Table Rock and Wiseman's View. The trail forks at 2.3 miles, marked by yellow tape; you should follow the yellow tape on a rhododendron, a second piece on a witch hazel, and a third piece on an umbrella magnolia. Just past the third piece of tape, a spur trail goes down to the left toward a swimming hole and the main trail continues to the right past more tape on a black birch. A tenth of a mile later, it approaches the river, where there is a great campsite. For the next 2 miles, you will gradually ascend away from the river and walk high above it. You will come to an overlook at 2.5 miles, where a rock perched 60 feet above the turbulent river looks out over a narrow point in the gorge. You will reach a campsite 0.2 mile later and another campsite 100 yards after that. The trail ascends on a switchback to the right at 3.2 miles, then veers sharply to the left. A tenth of a mile later, you will enter a horseshoe-shaped cove and cross a spring featuring lots of mossy rocks. An easily missed spur trail at 3.4 miles descends to join the Devil's Hole Trail (N 55' 1", W 54' 12"). The Linville Gorge Trail is high above the river at this point; the best way to find the junction is to continue 0.1 mile past the spring at 3.3 miles, then descend to the river and look for the Devil's Hole Creek on the other side. Almost 0.2 mile later, the Linville Gorge Trail meanders into and out of a series of ridge folds, over an ephemeral spring, and past a campsite. It crosses a brook, then continues high above the river; you will enjoy outstanding views of Hawksbill from an outcropping. You will reach a large camp-site in the middle of the trail at 3.8 miles, beneath a massive white pine and an enormous hemlock. Here, the Sandy Flats Trail forks off to the right (N 54' 43", W 54' 5"); there is a small waterfall 0.25 mile up the Sandy Flats Trail that is well worth the short detour. The Linville Gorge Trail continues straight ahead to another campsite. Two tenths of a mile later, it passes beneath a large rock overhang with a small campsite underneath. A tenth of a mile after that, it descends to a large riverside campsite. There is small spur trail to the left at 4.5 miles, marked by a piece of pink tape on a small hemlock. If you are looking for the Spence Ridge Trail, do not use this small spur trail; instead, you should continue 20 yards farther to the larger trail junction marked by an arrow carved into a white oak (N 54' 6", W 53' 51"). This spur trail switches back sharply to the left, descends to the river, and heads upstream 20 yards to a large, cube-shaped rock. This is probably the safest river crossing in the whole gorge—but note that even it is far from safe. Ahead, you will pass a Stonehenge-like structure with a campsite on top and a cave behind it. Fifty yards later, you will come to a small spring. A hundred yards later, you will reach another campsite beneath a rock overhang. There is a small campsite beside an Olympic pool–sized swimming hole at 5.3 miles. For the next 0.1 mile, you will pass a sequence of large campsites uphill to the right. The Conley Cove Trail forks off to the right at 5.5 miles beside a large campsite (N 53' 33", W 53' 54"). There are three large campsites in the next 0.1 mile; after that, the trail narrows. A massive rock outcropping descends to the river and a great swimming hole at 5.9 miles. Two tenths of a mile later, you will pass a similar rock formation that offers excellent views of the Chimneys to the south-southeast. For much of the rest of the trail, you will enjoy excellent views of Table Rock and the Chimneys across the river. The trail passes through a large hemlock grove at 6.3 miles, where you'll find a large campsite; there are two more campsites within the next 0.1

mile. After passing a cave beneath an overhang, you will cross a small spring at 6.8 miles. The small campsite 0.3 mile later offers excellent views of the Chimneys and Shortoff Mountain to the south. Thereafter, the trail, like the river valley, is wider, more gradual, and easier to negotiate. The trail crosses a winding spring at 8.2 miles and comes to a large campsite, where you'll see a red **G** with an arrow pointing diagonally to the north on a white oak and a red **G** with an arrow pointing straight up on a sweet gum. The Linville Gorge Trail forks to the right; a spur trail to the left heads toward a riverside campsite. Half a mile later, you'll come to a large campsite by the river, which is wide, shallow, and mellow at this point (N 51' 18", W 54' 4"). There is a faint trail on the other side of the river. If you are looking for the Cambric Branch Trail, you can try to wade here, then bushwhack 0.1 mile downstream to your right. The only other viable option is to continue 0.4 mile down the Linville Gorge Trail, cross the river at the boulders opposite Cambric Branch, then hike upriver 0.3 mile to the trailhead. The Linville Gorge Trail ascends away from the campsite, crosses a stream 50 yards later, and comes to another large campsite at 8.9 miles beneath enormous oak, beech, and hemlock. From here, you will veer to the right and begin a short but moderate ascent. Fifty yards later, you will pass an exceptionally thick white pine beside a massive boulder that juts out from the earth (N 51' 12", W 54' 5"). The complex folds of the quartz layers testify to the intense and ancient geologic history of the gorge. In front of the boulder, the Pinch-In Trail veers off to the right, marked by a small cairn in the middle of the trail; the Linville Gorge Trail drops to the left behind a large oak tree. When the Linville

Gorge Trail was created, it did not continue beyond here, but veered off to the right on what is now called the Pinch-In Trail. Even today, few people continue beyond this point on the Linville Gorge Trail, which becomes a mixture of overlapping spur trails beneath poplar, elm, alder, beech, and hickory as it winds its way south for another 2 miles. Unfortunately, tasteless imbeciles have taken to dumping staggering amounts of trash along the way. The trail ends at private property. It is impossible to continue farther downstream to join the Mountains-to-Sea Trail as it descends from Pinnacle, crosses the Linville River, then ascends Shortoff Mountain.

PINE GAP TRAIL

Length: 0.7 mile one way
Difficulty: easy
Elevation change: 200 feet
USGS quadrant: Linville Falls
Access: From N.C. 183, turn south on Kistler Memorial Highway and drive 0.7 mile to the parking area on the left, where a wooden sign marks the trailhead (N 35° 56' 23", W 81° 55' 49").

This is the northernmost and easiest of the West Rim trails. The Linville Gorge Trail begins at the Pine Gap Trail's terminus. The Pine Gap Trail follows an easy descent on a narrow path lined with galax, rhododendron, mountain laurel, and some truly massive hemlock trees. It switches back after 0.2 mile, then again 0.2 mile later. After 0.5 mile, look for pink tape on a rhododendron beside a large stump and for a fallen tree immediately to the right. There is a good campsite 10 yards to your left, marked by red tape on a rhododendron; the river is ten yards beyond that. The Pine Gap Trail continues behind the fallen tree and begins a moderate ascent beneath large rock overhangs to the right. After 100 yards, the river is no longer visible. At 0.7 mile, the trail bends to the right and ends at an intersection (N 56' 16", W 55' 11"). The Bynum Bluff Trail extends to the right and left; the Linville Gorge Trail begins straight ahead.

The wide trail begins an easy ridge route through doghobble, mountain laurel, hemlock, galax, and various oaks. After 100 yards, you will pass several campsites. For the next 0.2 mile, you will pass a few choice spur trails to the right that lead to spectacular views of the gorge to the southeast. The trail narrows after 0.3 mile and passes among white pine and lots of the fascinating and rare turkey beard. A tenth of a mile later, it switches back sharply to the right and begins a moderate descent; this turn is often missed, since a spur trail continues straight ahead. For the next 0.25 mile, you will negotiate a series of switchbacks. The trail levels out at a good campsite at 0.8 mile. Fifty yards later, it intersects the Linville Gorge Trail, marked by remnants of an old sign with orange tape. Continue straight ahead. The trail drops steeply to the right 0.2 mile later and makes a rapid descent to the river. You will reach the river at 1.2 miles at the site of a large campsite, a swimming hole, and a small waterfall. Across the river are the cliffs of Brushy Ridge.

CABIN TRAIL (#246)

Length: 0.6 mile one way
Difficulty: very strenuous
Elevation change: 800 feet
USGS quadrant: Linville Falls
Access: From N.C. 183, drive 1.8 miles down Kistler
    Memorial Highway to the parking area on the left,
    where a wooden sign marks the trailhead (N 35° 55'
    38", W 81° 55' 31"). See maps on pages 122–123.

This little-used trail is the shortest and one of the two steepest on the West Rim. It is *very* steep. The first 50 yards make an easy descent through beech, white oak, Solomon's-seal, and lady fern. Soon thereafter, you will begin a strenuous descent through rhododendron and hemlock. There is a small campsite beneath a large hemlock at 0.3 mile; just past the campsite is a nice view of Hawksbill to the east. The trail ends at its junction with the Linville Gorge Trail after 0.6 mile. Note: If you are coming from the Linville Gorge Trail, this trail junction is easily missed. Look for "C-A-B-I-N" carved into a 12-inch red maple and a rectangular rock with two arrows scratched into it; the trail begins after you scramble over some large, exposed rocks.

BABEL TOWER TRAIL (#240)

Length: 1.4 miles one way
Difficulty: moderate to strenuous
Elevation change: 875 feet
USGS quadrant: Linville Falls
Access: From N.C. 183, drive 2.6 miles down Kistler
　　　　Memorial Highway to the parking area on the left,
　　　　where a wooden sign marks the trailhead (N 35° 55'
　　　　6", W 81° 55' 10"). See maps on pages 122–123.

This very popular and heavily used trail descends to a massive rock formation that presumably got its name from the resemblance of the complex rock fissures to a tower of haphazardly stacked bricks reaching to the heavens. The broad trail begins with an easy descent through mountain laurel, galax, and poison ivy beneath a mixed hardwood canopy. You will reach large campsites after 100 yards and a small spring 50 yards later. Soon thereafter, you will pass beneath several massive hemlock trees. There is a small campsite downhill to the left at 0.5 mile, after a series of switchbacks. The decent becomes moderate 0.3 mile later as it passes through blueberry, sumac, white pine, goldenrod, and mountain gentian. You will descend to a small saddle at 1.2 miles, where the Linville Gorge Trail drops to the left and right. The Babel Tower Trail continues straight ahead toward the rock outcroppings. If you look to the left as you ascend the rocks, you will see the Linville River flowing north as it snakes around Babel Tower. From here, the trail descends to the right, skirts to the left of the cliffs, then scrambles to a rock exposure near the summit. Standing atop the rocky precipice, you will be surrounded by bristly locust, mountain laurel, white and pitch pine, blueberry, Carolina hemlock, and black cherry. You will enjoy outstanding views of the cliffs of Sitting Bear Mountain at 97° and 1.1 miles, Hawksbill at 136° and 1.8 miles, Table Rock at 155° and 3.1 miles, the Chimneys at 170° and 3.9 miles, and Wiseman's View at 175° and 1.8 miles.

SANDY FLATS TRAIL (#230)

Length: 1 mile one way
Difficulty: very strenuous
Elevation change: 1,200 feet
USGS quadrant: Linville Falls
Access: From N.C. 183, drive 3.7 miles down Kistler
    Memorial Highway to the parking area on the left,
    where a wooden sign marks the trailhead (N 35° 54'
    24", W 81° 54' 40"). See maps on pages 122–123.

This is a trail for the hiking masochist. Sandwiched between the comparatively mellow Babel Tower Trail to the north and Conley Cove Trail to the south, it is perhaps the steepest and most difficult trail in the entire gorge, and therefore in the entire national forest. You should attempt this primitive trail only if you enjoy a challenge.

The trail follows a moderate descent through rhododendron along a heavily washed-out path. After 0.5 mile, it rounds a corner to the right, where you'll enjoy excellent views of Hawksbill in front and Wiseman's View to the right. The trail switches back, crosses a spring, and comes to a difficult-to-negotiate rock escarpment after 0.6 mile. There is no easy route down the rockface; the descent can be dangerous with a heavy pack. At the bottom of the escarpment, you will proceed alongside a large, fallen hemlock toward some orange tape on a rhododendron. At 1 mile, the trail proceeds atop a large, exposed rock;

it resumes near the orange tape to the right at the bottom. From here, you will walk alongside a beautiful spring that runs through a moss-covered rock channel. A tenth of a mile later, you will reach a spur trail to the right that leads to a serendipitous waterfall; the water drops 15 feet off of a moss-covered rock ledge. Two tenths of a mile later, the trail makes a sharp left turn marked by orange tape on an umbrella magnolia and blue tape on a rhododendron; a spur trail forks off to the right. The trail ends 100 yards later at a large campsite beneath a massive white pine and a hemlock on the Linville Gorge Trail. Note: If you are coming from the Linville Gorge Trail, this junction is easily missed. When you reach the large campsite in the middle of the trail beneath a massive white pine and a hemlock, you should fork to the west (right, if you are descending downstream).

CONLEY COVE TRAIL (#229)

Length: 1.4 miles one way
Difficulty: moderate to strenuous
Elevation change: 1,050 feet
USGS quadrant: Linville Falls
Access: From N.C. 183, drive 5.3 miles down Kistler
Memorial Highway to the parking area on the left,
where a wooden sign marks the trailhead (N 35° 53'
23", W 81° 54' 22"). See maps on pages 122–123.

This popular hike begins on a wide, easy path through mountain laurel, chestnut oak, Carolina silverbell, white pine, sourwood, black gum, and galax. After 0.2 mile, the primitive Rock Jock Trail forks off to the right; straight ahead, the Conley Cove Trail begins a long series of moderate switchbacks beneath rhododendron, hemlock, and occasional chestnut oak stumps. At 0.5 mile, it passes alongside a massive rock wall to a cavelike overhang and campsite. You will then descend a continuous series of switchbacks through Solomon's-seal, rhododendron, spiderwort, fire pink, baneberry, beardtongue, foamflower, viburnum, bloodroot, blue cohosh, whorled loosestrife, and mountain bugbane. There are excellent views of Table Rock directly across the gorge. Just prior to the 1.5-mile mark, the trail ends at a campsite on the Linville Gorge Trail. Note: If you are descending the Linville Gorge Trail, you will come to a small campsite in the middle of the trail and a larger campsite uphill to the right after 5.5 miles. Just ahead, the Conley Cove Trail forks to the right beside a large hemlock; the fork is marked by orange tape on a rhododendron.

PINCH-IN TRAIL (#228)

Length: 1.4 miles one way
Difficulty: very strenuous
Elevation change: 1700 feet
USGS quadrant: Ashford
Access: From N.C. 183, drive 8.5 miles down Kistler Memorial Highway to the parking area on the left, where a wooden sign marks the trailhead (N 35° 51' 3", W 81° 55' 3"). See maps on pages 122–123.

The trail begins on a wide path that narrows after 50 yards as it starts a strenuous descent through white pine and oak. The trail makes a sharp right turn at 0.4 mile, marked by a small cairn in the trail and orange tape on a mountain laurel; straight ahead, spur trails veer off to some spectacular views of the cliffs of Shortoff Mountain to the right and the Chimneys to the left.

A tenth of a mile later, you will descend to a large rock outcropping where the trail veers to the left. For the next 0.5 mile, the trail steeply descends the spine of the ridge; you will have to negotiate frequent, short switchbacks. The trail mellows to a mere moderate-to-strenuous descent after 1 mile. You will come to a faint spur trail to the right at 1.1 miles. Fifty yards later, the trail crosses a small gulch and comes to a second, more substantial fork marked by orange tape on a hemlock. The Pinch-In Trail continues to the left; the spur trail to the right connects with one of the many spur trails along the Linville Gorge Trail. About 30 yards later, the Pinch-In Trail ends beneath an enormous boulder at the junction with the Linville Gorge Trail (N 51' 12", W 54' 5").

Several loop options are available on the West Rim of Linville Gorge. All of them involve walking a considerable stretch on Kistler Memorial Highway. Two of the more popular loops are described below.

WEST RIM LOOP #1
Length: 2.2 miles
Difficulty: moderate
Elevation change: 500 feet
USGS quadrant: Linville Falls

Take the Pine Gap Trail to its end, then turn right on the Bynum Bluff Trail. When you return to the dirt road, turn right; it is 0.7 mile to the beginning of the loop.

WEST RIM LOOP #2
Length: 7.4 miles
Difficulty: strenuous
Elevation change: 2,000 feet
USGS quadrant: Linville Falls

Descend the Babel Tower Trail to the Linville Gorge Trail and turn right. Three and one-half miles later, turn right on the Conley Cove Trail. When you return to the dirt road, turn right; it is 2.7 miles back to the starting point.

EAST RIM TRAILS

All but one of the trails on the East Rim of Linville Gorge begin off the same dirt road. From N.C. 181 some 3 miles south of the N.C. 183, turn on to Gingercake Road. Note that Gingercake Road is a loop road; if you are coming down N.C. 181 from the north, take the *second* turn for Gingercake Road. The road forks after 0.3 mile. Gingercake Road continues to the right; Table Rock Road begins to the left. The Brushy Ridge Trail is located off Gingercake Road, and the other trails begin off Table Rock Road. Nine tenths of a mile after the fork on Table Rock Road, the pavement ends and F.R. 210 begins. When the road forks 4.7 miles later, turn right on F.R. 210B. You will pass the Outward Bound School to the right. The road soon becomes paved again. It ends at a large parking area with restrooms but no water.

From where the pavement ends and F.R. 210 begins, it is 1.6 miles to the Devil's Hole Trail, 2.7 miles to the Hawksbill and Jonas Ridge Trails, 3.6 miles to the Spence Ridge and Table

Rock Gap Trails, and 7.7 miles to the Table Rock Summit, Little Table Rock, Shortoff Mountain, and Cambric Branch Trails.

BRUSHY RIDGE TRAIL (#232)

Length: up to 2.1 miles one way
Difficulty: easy to moderate for the first mile, strenuous thereafter
Elevation change: up to 800 feet
USGS quadrant: Linville Falls
Access: From N.C. 181 some 3 miles south of its junction with N.C. 183 in the Jonas Ridge community, turn on to Gingercake Road (turn right if you are heading down the mountain). At 0.3 mile, bear right at the first fork in the road. At 0.9 mile, you will see a sign for Mountain Park Road on the left beside two parallel roads; take the second (the higher) of the roads. Follow Mountain Park Road for 1 mile to an intersection. To the left, the road loops back down to Gingercake Road; to the right, it continues up the hill to private residences. There is limited parking here; be sure not to block any of the driveways at this loop. The footpath begins behind the small rock wall to the right (N 35° 56' 35", W 81° 53' 48"). See maps on pages 122–123.

The trail begins on an old roadbed. After 100 yards, you will cross a small spring descending from the right; a sign here indicates the Pisgah National Forest property boundary. The roadbed then narrows as it passes beneath a dense canopy of rhododendron. The trail begins an easy-to-moderate ascent after 0.25 mile, passing through a diverse forest of chestnut oak, sassafras, witch hazel, galax, mountain laurel, hemlock, white oak, white pine, partridgeberry, maple, umbrella magnolia, sourwood, ground cedar, beech, rosy twisted-stalk, and oak fern. At 1 mile, the roadbed ends and a narrow footpath continues straight ahead (N 56' 24", W 54' 37"). Shortly thereafter, the trail begins a moderate ascent of a small knob. It crests the knob 0.1 mile later. You will negotiate a short, strenuous ascent and descent before reaching a small clearing at 1.2 miles (N 56' 15", W 54' 50"). To the right is a small rock outcropping from which you will enjoy an excellent view to the west of Humpback Mountain and the Blue Ridge. Past the overlook, the trail makes a strenuous descent of the ridge spine. After 0.3 mile, it reaches a small rock jutting into the middle of the trail among white and pitch pine, Eastern and Carolina hemlock, downy service-berry, and mountain laurel (N 56' 7", W 55' 2"). From this rock, you will enjoy unparalleled views to the south down the gorge. The cliffs of Bynum Bluff are visible at 275° and 0.25 mile, Babel Tower at 138° and 0.5 mile, Hawksbill at 137° and 2.3 miles, and Table Rock at 153° and 3.6 miles. For most hikers, this is the end of the trail; however, the trail does continue for another 0.6 mile in an extremely rough, wild, and strenuous fashion. It descends steeply to the right to a small saddle and a campsite, scrambles past some fascinating, complex rock formations, ascends a small knob, then descends (plummets, actually) to a bend in Linville River at 2.1 miles (N 55' 58", W 55' 30"). If you're considering trying to cross the river here to join the Linville Gorge Trail, good luck! The river isn't particularly deep or fast at this bend, but the Linville Gorge Trail is high up the opposite ridge, and there is no clear, safe scramble to reach it. Thus, your best bet is to backtrack.

HAWKSBILL TRAIL (#217)
Length: 0.7 mile one way
Difficulty: strenuous
Elevation change: 850 feet
USGS quadrant: Linville Falls
Access: There is a parking area on the left on F.R. 210
 some 2.7 miles after the pavement ends. The
 trailhead is on the right (N 35° 54' 52", W 81° 52'
 43"). See maps on pages 122–123.

The trail begins in a steep, washed-out gulch lined with rhododendron, oak fern, mountain laurel, mountain gentian, blueberry, bush pea, galax, hemlock, and witch hazel. The ascent is strenuous for the first 0.25 mile, then becomes moderate for the next 0.25 mile. After 0.5 mile, you'll come to an intersection where a chestnut tree and a large signpost stand in the middle of the trail; an arrow carved into the signpost points to the left (N 54' 55", W 53' 10"). Straight ahead begins the Jonas Ridge Trail. Despite the arrow, the trail to the left is not the main route up Hawksbill; the main trail begins about 5 yards prior to the intersection and ascends steeply to the left. Two tenths of a mile later, you will reach the summit, where there is a small, flat area too rocky for comfortable camping (N 54' 47", W 53' 10"). From here, multiple spur trails radiate outward to

Table Rock (left) and Hawksbill
PHOTO BY CAROLYN SAKOWSKI

various overlooks. The numerous pitch pine and Pierus trees at the summit have been dwarfed by the harsh elements, creating a bonsai-esque landscape. The panorama from the summit is astounding. Beginning to the south, you will see Table Rock at 179° and 1.5 miles, Shortoff Mountain at 192° and 5.1 miles, Woods Mountain at 236° and 14.7 miles, Wiseman's View at 243° and 1.2 miles, Mount Mitchell at 249° and 23.5 miles, Yellow Mountain at 303° and 11 miles, Babel Tower at 371° and 1.9 miles, Headquarters Mountain at 10° and 5.6 miles, Grandfather Mountain at 22° and 14.3 miles, Chestnut Mountain at 58° and 5.5 miles, Brown Mountain at 86° and 7.3 miles, and Brandy Cove Mountain at 124° and 2.6 miles.

JONAS RIDGE TRAIL (#245)

Length: 2.2 miles one way
Difficulty: easy to moderate, with one very strenuous section
Elevation change: 650 feet
USGS quadrant: Linville Falls
Access: The trailhead is off the Hawksbill Trail (N 54' 55", W 53' 10"). Drive 2.7 miles down F.R. 210 to the Hawksbill Parking Lot, then follow the Hawksbill Trail for 0.5 mile to the wooden signpost. Continue straight ahead from there. See maps on pages 122–123.

There is a campsite on the right 15 yards past the wooden post. The trail begins a moderate ascent of a small knob beneath a tight canopy of mountain laurel and rhododendron. It descends to a flat area after 0.6 mile, where it forks. To the right, the trail descends 0.2 mile to the Devil's Hole Parking Area; the main trail continues to a massive campsite beneath several hickory trees (N 55' 18", W 53' 19"). For the next 0.2 mile, the Jonas Ridge Trail and the Devil's Hole Trail run conjunctively. Just past the campsite are a wooden Forest Service sign, a small campsite to the left, and a small spur trail that breaks off to the right; this trail, too, goes to the Devil's Hole Parking Area and should be avoided. From here, the trail descends to a saddle and a beautiful grove of white pine with occasional hemlock, sassafras, wood fern, mock strawberry, ground cedar, and wood betony; an old rock wall runs parallel to the trail on the left. About 30 yards north of the saddle, the Devil's Hole Trail breaks off to the left, marked by a wooden sign and blue tape on a witch hazel and a mountain laurel (N 55' 26", W 53' 21"). The Jonas Ridge Trail then narrows considerably and begins a moderate-to-strenuous ascent along an open hillside featuring goldenrod, aster, white snakeroot, and meadow rue beneath a mixed hardwood canopy. Around 1.1 miles, after a strenuous ascent, the trail switches back sharply to the left and scrambles to the spine of the ridge; a short spur trail to the left leads to an incredible view of Babel Tower across the gorge. Fifty yards later, you will approach what is perhaps the most bizarre and fascinating rock formation in the entire national forest—a massive rock monolith, reminiscent of the mesas of the Southwest in its angular austerity, juts out of the ground. The trail continues a very strenuous ascent of the ridge for 0.1 mile before reaching a plateau at the top of Sitting Bear Mountain, where there is a good campsite beneath a white oak. A short spur trail forks left to the spectacular cliffs of Sitting Bear Mountain, where you can enjoy outstanding views of Babel Tower and Wiseman's View. From the campsite, you will make an easy-to-moderate ascent past lots of sourwood, striped maple, witch hazel, and club moss. After 50 yards, you will reach a second campsite to the right that offers excellent views to the east of Chestnut Mountain at 70° and 5.1 miles, Brown Mountain at 96° and 7.4 miles, and Brandy Cove Mountain at 140° and 3.5 miles. The trail continues through a tight, narrow tunnel of mountain laurel and begins an easy descent off Sitting Bear Mountain 0.1 mile later. The westbound spur trail on the left at 1.6 miles doesn't go anywhere; the main trail continues north on a wide and flat course atop Gingercake Mountain. It descends to a large, flat area at 2.2 miles (N 56' 25", W 53' 16"). This former cabin site marks the end of the trail, as the roadbed to the left descends to private property.

DEVIL'S HOLE TRAIL (#244)
Length: 1.5 miles one way
Difficulty: strenuous
Elevation change: 1,200 feet
USGS quadrant: Linville Falls
Access: From the end of the pavement on F.R. 210, it is 1.6 miles to the trailhead, where there is limited parking. The wooden Forest Service sign here does not indicate the Devil's Hole Trail (N 35° 55' 21", W 81° 53' 14"). See maps on pages 122–123.

You will begin to the right of a small spring and head southwest up a narrow and easy-to-moderate path. After twenty yards, a smaller trail forks off to the right; you should avoid this trail, as the two run parallel to the same destination. The trail passes through a lovely, young forest of yellow birch, sourwood, black gum, dogwood, white snakeroot, purple-crested dwarf iris, violets, Clinton's lily, and ground cedar. Less than 0.2 mile later, it comes to a T intersection with the Jonas Ridge Trail. To the left, it is 0.8 mile to the summit of Hawksbill; to the right, two trails run conjunctively for the next 0.2 mile. The trail passes a very large campsite beneath several hickory trees. Just past the campsite are a wooden Forest Service sign, a small campsite to the left, and the small spur trail mentioned earlier. The trail then descends to a saddle and a beautiful grove of white pine with occasional hemlock, sassafras, wood fern, mock strawberry, ground cedar, and wood betony. An old rock wall runs parallel to the trail on the left. About 30 yards north of the saddle, the Devil's Hole Trail breaks off to the left, marked by a wooden sign and blue tape on a witch hazel and a mountain laurel; the Jonas Ridge Trail continues straight ahead (N 55' 26", W 53' 21"). The Devil's Hole Trail begins a strenuous descent of a narrow path lined with sassafras, rhododendron, witch hazel, mountain laurel, white and chestnut oak, mountain gentian, wood aster, goldenrod, and foamflower. After 0.5 mile, the grade becomes more moderate as you descend into a steep-walled ravine containing an old-growth forest with several enormous hemlock and oak trees. You will pass a piece of pink tape on a dead rhododendron, several boulders positively dripping with moss, and a remarkable, hollowed-out hemlock so large that you can walk through it. The trail is extremely faint as it snakes its way down the ravine; there is a plethora of cairns, however, to help guide the way. The trail veers to the right after 1 mile and approaches Devil's Hole Creek. To the left, another stream cascades off a moss-covered shelf surrounded by several enormous hemlock trees. Fifty yards later, the two streams combine. The trail crosses them just upstream from a small waterfall and pool. A hundred yards later, you will cross again, so that the creek is now to your right. The trail enters a small campsite at 1.4 miles, where you'll see a large, rectangular rock with quartzite veins shining through layers of moss and clinging ferns. Fifty yards later, you'll come to an incredible campsite overlooking the Linville River. From here, the trail drops to the left past a small campsite and scrambles down the riverbank (N 55' 1", W 54' 9"). To the left, the river shelf drops 8 feet, creating a terrific rapid. Devil's Hole Creek flows in 100 yards upstream. A hundred yards farther upstream, there is a series of boulders in the river; this is probably the best place to cross if you are trying to reach the Linville Gorge Trail.

SPENCE RIDGE TRAIL (#233)

Length: 1.7 miles one way
Difficulty: moderate
Elevation change: 650 feet
USGS quadrant: Linville Falls
Access: The eastern trailhead is on F.R. 210 some 3.6
   miles south of where the pavement ends; there is a
   large parking area on the left and a clearly labeled
   sign on the right (N 35° 54' 13", W 81° 52' 45"). The
   western trailhead is on the western bank of the Linville
   River (N 35° 54' 6", W 81° 53' 50"). See maps on
   pages 122–123.

This is one of the most popular trails in Linville Gorge, partly because it offers the easiest to access to the river from the eastern side of the river and is the most commonly used trail to cross the river. The trail begins on a straight, wide roadbed beneath hemlock and rhododendron. After 100 yards, you will pass a registration stand and begin a moderate descent. Four tenths of a mile later, the trail reaches a flat area and a trail junction. The Little Table Rock Trail forks off to the left; the Spence Ridge Trail switches back sharply to the right (N 54' 3", W 53' 9"). From here, the trail narrows and becomes rockier. It switches back sharply to the left at 0.7 mile and passes alongside a branch; across the branch is a good campsite. A tenth of a mile later, the trail rock-hops the stream beneath a dense, lush canopy of rhododendron, passes a couple of campsites, and rock-hops a second branch among lots of pipsissewa, club moss, Christmas fern, and witch hazel. You will enter an old-growth hemlock forest peppered with huge boulders around 1.2 miles. About 0.1 mile later, the trail switches back several times and moves alongside the creek past an lovely cascade and pool near a campsite. After a series of short, moderate-to-strenuous switchbacks, you will descend to the Linville River. To the right is a massive swimming pool; directly across is a large, flat boulder in the middle of the river. This boulder is the most commonly used crossing point to reach the Linville Trail on the other side. However, the crossing is far from easy. In fact, it can be very dangerous if the water level is high—especially if you're wearing a backpack. On the other side of the river, the trail heads downstream briefly before ascending the bank.

If you're trying to find the Spence Ridge Trail from the Linville River Trail, look for an arrow pointing to the left carved into a white oak. Descend this spur trail and go upstream several yards to the massive, flat boulder in the middle of the river. Once you are on the other side of the river, you will see a small creek flow into the river to your right. The Spence Ridge Trail begins to the left of the creek, surrounded by alder, red maple, rue anemone, blackberry, dog-hobble, mountain laurel, and doll's eye.

TABLE ROCK GAP TRAIL (#243)

Length: 1.5 miles one way
Difficulty: strenuous
Elevation change: 700 feet
USGS quadrant: Linville Falls
Access: The main trailhead is located immediately to the left of the Spence Ridge Trail 3.6 miles south of F.R. 210 (N 35° 54' 13", W 81° 52' 45"). The trail ends at its junction with the Table Rock Summit Trail (N 35° 53' 27", W 81° 53' 6"). See maps on pages 122–123.

Immediately to the left of the Spence Ridge Trial, you will see an old logging road running parallel to the main road; the logging road runs beside a wooden sign reading, "210." The trail follows the gravel roadbed for 0.4 mile to a large, grassy clearing. To the left, two white dots on a tulip poplar indicate the junction with the Mountains-to-Sea Trail. The old road continues straight ahead; the Table Rock Gap Trail follows the Mountains-to-Sea Trail as it forks to the right, passes a white dot on a tulip poplar, and begins a strenuous ascent.

View from the base of Table Rock
PHOTO BY CAROLYN SAKOWSKI

Three tenths of a mile later, after a brutal ascent and a series of switchbacks, the trail approaches a boulder field and a large rock overhang. It then mellows to a moderate ascent on a very narrow, tight path guarded by rhododendron. To the right, you will be treated to increasingly frequent glimpses of the remarkable gorge. At 1.4 miles, you will cross a small spring descending from the left. You will then reach a small spur trail to the left. A tenth of a mile later, the trail ends at its junction with the Table Rock Summit Trail, marked by a wooden signpost. It is 0.3 mile to the summit, 0.4 mile to the Table Rock Parking Area, and less than 0.1 mile to the Little Table Rock Trail.

LITTLE TABLE ROCK TRAIL (#236)

Length: 1.2 miles one way
Difficulty: strenuous
Elevation change: 1,000 feet
USGS quadrant: Linville Falls
Access: This trail can be reached by either of two trails.
   The northern trailhead is at a switchback on the
   Spence Ridge Trail (N 35° 54' 3", W 81° 53' 9") some
   0.4 mile from the parking area on F.R. 210. The
   southern trailhead is in a small saddle on the Table
   Rock Summit Trail (N 35° 53' 23", W 81° 53' 10")
   some 0.3 mile north of the Table Rock Parking Area.
   See maps on pages 122–123.

This is a seldom-used, primitive, and rough trail. From the saddle in the Table Rock Summit Trail, the Little Table Rock Trail branches off perpendicularly to the left. Forty yards later, it forks at the summit of Little Table Rock. The trail to the left goes to a campsite; the Little Table Rock Trail begins its descent ahead to the right. For the next 0.75 mile, it descends very

View of Table Rock with Linville Gorge on the right
PHOTO BY CAROLYN SAKOWSKI

steeply to the north through a dense forest of mixed hardwoods. You will cross a beautiful, rushing creek after 0.9 mile. On the other side of the creek, the trail joins an old roadbed and follows it to the right. There are no blazes to mark this confusing intersection; look for a large locust and an umbrella magnolia. (Note: If you are coming from the opposite direction, this turn is easily missed. The roadbed makes a sharp bend to the right, but the trail continues straight across the creek.)

The trail follows the roadbed to the top of a ridge, then descends to the right. After a brief descent, you will pass a large campsite near another creek, then turn to the right. About 30 yards later, the trail crosses the creek. It ascends on another roadbed to a large campsite 50 yards later. A spur trail forks off to the left; the main trail bends to the right and begins a moderate ascent on an overgrown roadbed. Shortly thereafter, it emerges from a dense rhododendron thicket to a campsite in the middle of a wide roadbed. From here, you will follow an easy path through a grove of young white pine and hemlock for 0.1 mile, whereupon the trail ends at the junction with the Spence Ridge Trail.

TABLE ROCK SUMMIT TRAIL (#242)

Length: 0.7 mile one way
Difficulty: moderate to strenuous
Elevation change: 550 feet
USGS quadrant: Linville Falls
Access: From N.C. 181 some 3 miles south of N.C. 183, turn on to Gingercake Road. After 0.3 mile, turn left on Table Rock Road. The pavement ends 0.9 mile later, at which point the road becomes F.R. 210. Drive 4.7 miles from where the pavement ends, then turn right on F.R. 210B. Three miles later, you'll arrive at the large, paved parking area just south of the summit (N 35° 53' 11", W 81° 53' 5"). See maps on pages 122–123.

This is one of the most popular hikes in the national forest, so don't come here expecting solitude. The trail runs conjunctively with a section of the Mountains-to-Sea Trail, so there are frequent white blazes.

The trail begins at the northern end of the parking area, past a large wooden display board. After 100 yards, you will begin a strenuous ascent of a wide, rocky path. You will come to a T intersection at 0.3 mile (N 53' 23", W 53' 10"). The Little Table Rock Trail begins to the left; the Table Rock Summit Trail switches back to the right. One hundred yards later, you will reach a wooden sign and a fork in the trail. The Mountains-to-Sea Trail forks to the right, following the Table Rock Gap Trail;

the Table Rock Summit Trail continues straight ahead. From here, the trail follows a series of short switchbacks until reaching the summit 0.3 mile later. From the summit, you will see Hawksbill due north at 1.5 miles, Sugar Mountain and its loathsome high-rise at 7° and 16.2 miles, Grandfather Mountain at 20° and 15.7 miles, Yancey Ridge at 37° and 11.7 miles, Chestnut Mountain (on the border of Burke, Avery, and Caldwell Counties) at 46° and 6.5 miles, Brown Mountain at 74° and 7.5 miles, Chestnut Mountain (in Caldwell County) at 98° and 24.3 miles, Swayback Knob at 166° and 20 miles, Marlin Knob at 180° and 26.5 miles, Shortoff Mountain at 198° and 4 miles, Woods Mountain at 241° and 13.9 miles, Mount Mitchell at 253° and 23.1 miles, Woodys Knob at 272° and 12.4 miles, "Table Rock #3" at 289° and 5.6 miles, Spear Tops at 318° and 11.8 miles, Laurel Knob at 320° and 2.5 miles (with Doe Hill directly behind it at 7.5 miles), Big Yellow Mountain at 337° and 16.9 miles, and Long Arm Mountain at 354° and 4.8 miles.

SHORTOFF MOUNTAIN TRAIL (#235)

Length: 6 miles one way
Difficulty: strenuous
Elevation change: 1,000 feet
USGS quadrants: Linville Falls, Ashford, Oak Hill
Access: The Table Rock Parking Lot is located 7.7 miles down F.R. 210. The trail begins beside the restrooms at the southern end of the parking lot (N 35° 53' 11", W 81° 53' 5"). See maps on pages 122–123.

This is one of the most popular full-day hikes in Pisgah National Forest, and understandably so. The trail offers a sustained tour along the southern half of the East Rim of Linville Gorge and includes such geological highlights as the Chimneys and the many cliffs of Shortoff Mountain. It also runs conjunctively with a section of the Mountains-to-Sea Trail, so it is frequently blazed with the ubiquitous white dot; in fact, it is probably the "most blazed" trail in the entire gorge. If you are not interested in hiking the full 6 miles, it is highly recommended that you hike as far as the overlook at 1.3 miles.

The trail begins on a wide path, heading south past several picnic tables beneath white pine, chestnut oak, striped maple, and rhododendron. A tenth of mile later, it leaves the picnic area and narrows considerably. The numerous rock outcroppings to the left offer outstanding views to the southeast of the Piedmont and the South Mountains. After 0.5 mile, you will reach an overlook that provides an incredible view to the west and south. From here, the trail descends through a series of narrow, often tricky rocky crevasses toward the Chimneys. In addition to being a haven for rock-climbing enthusiasts, the Chimneys are the site of one of the nation's first successful peregrine falcon reintroduction efforts; the pair of falcons nests in the Chimneys and occasionally can be seen hunting nearby. After passing through a dense, narrow laurel slick, you will leave the Chimneys at 0.9 mile; there is a nice campsite on the left. The trail begins an easy-to-moderate descent through downy serviceberry, blueberry, Pierus, oak fern, white pine, hemlock, white snakeroot, chestnut oak, witch hazel, mountain laurel, and the rare Heller's blazing star and mountain golden heather. It drops to the left, passes through an old, burned-out clearing of table mountain pine and sourwood at 1.3 miles, and switches back to the right; straight ahead are spectacular views of Table

The view from Shortoff in Linville Gorge includes Lake James

Rock at 14° and 1.3 miles, Winding Star Knob on Ripshin Ridge
at 21° and 6.3 miles, Brown Mountain at 66° and 8.2 miles,
Ironmonger Mountain at 135° and 18.7 miles, and Wilson Creek
Valley to the east. You will then make a strenuous descent on a
narrow, eroded path. You will crest two small knobs with campsites after 0.4 mile and 0.6 mile before reaching Chimney Gap
at 2 miles, where there is a large campsite beneath chestnut
oak, red oak, and white pine. From here, the trail begins a strenuous ascent. After 200 yards, a spur trail forks off to the left and
heads toward a small spring. You will pass an entire hillside
blanketed with galax before cresting a small ridge at 2.3 miles
(N 51' 36", W 52' 50"), where there is a confusing intersection
marked by a white blaze on a sourwood and two white dots
on a black oak. The Shortoff Mountain Trail forks left; straight

ahead begins the Cambric Branch Trail. For the next 0.75 mile, the trail curves east, then south as it wraps around Cambric Cove. The series of moderate descents and ascents is lined with black birch, Carolina basswood, striped maple, mountain gentian, dogwood, moosewood, lady's-slipper, Solomon's-seal, squaw-corn, and flame azalea. You will reach the first of many outstanding overlooks at 3.1 miles; a spur trail to the right goes toward a small rock outcropping that offers an excellent view of Table Rock directly north. After a moderate ascent 0.25 mile later, the trail passes a large boulder to the right at the highest point on Shortoff Mountain, then begins a moderate descent. It passes a small campsite to the left at 4.3 miles. A tenth of a mile later, it comes to the second spectacular overlook, a former burn sight with lots of pitch pine, table mountain pine, blueberry, hemlock, rhododendron, and goldenrod. After 4.8 miles, you will reach a third overlook, where the trail forks. The right fork begins an 0.25-mile loop alongside the cliffs; straight ahead, the main trail continues beneath a high canopy of black gum and other hardwoods. Looking to the north, you will see Grandfather Mountain at 19° and 19.4 miles, Table Rock at 16° and 3.6 miles, Hawksbill at 11° and 5.1 miles, the Chimneys at 10° and 2.5 miles, Wiseman's View at 358° and 4.5 miles, Big Yellow Mountain at 344° and 19.8 miles, Little Yellow Mountain at 333° and 18.2 miles, Spear Tops at 330° and 14.1 miles, Mount Mitchell at 261° and 21.2 miles, and Woods Mountain at 253° and 11.5 miles. The loop trail reconnects after 0.1 mile. A tenth of a mile later, the trail passes to the left of a large, circular clearing. Rain often collects into a large pool here, at which times the clearing becomes a watering hole for local fauna;

hikers frequently find deer, raccoon, and bear tracks imprinted in the mud. On the western side of the circle, you might find a small spur trail that leads to a large rock overhang. With some skill, it is possible to climb beneath the overhang. In winter, it is possible to see icicles 10 to 20 feet long hanging off the rocks. Continue 20 yards past the circle on the main trail, where a spur trail breaks off to the left and leads to a series of campsites. At 5.3 miles, you will come to a large intersection marked by a red oak stripped of bark and a large wooden signpost buried in the dirt (N 49' 58", W 53' 55"). The Shortoff Mountain Trail and the Mountains-to-Sea Trail break off perpendicularly to the right; the sandy, rocky roadbed straight ahead descends steeply, reconnects with the Mountains-to-Sea Trail after 0.3 mile, and continues down to the Linville River 1.5 miles after that. The Shortoff Mountain Trail comes to a fourth incredible overlook 0.2 mile past the intersection. To the west, you will see Dobson Knob at 254° and 5.1 miles, Mackey Mountain at 243° and 16 miles, Marlin Knob at 176° and 22.6 miles, and Swayback Knob at 158° and 16.8 miles. From here, the trail follows a serpentine route south past several small rock formations. There are numerous spur trails along the way; in order to lessen the erosion, please avoid them. Half a mile later, the Shortoff Mountain Trail ends at a T intersection with the dirt roadbed mentioned above; the intersection is marked by two white dots on an old pine. Straight ahead, a roadbed descends to private property and Wolf Pit Road. To the left, it is 5.6 miles to Table Rock. To the right, it is 1.5 miles on the Mountains-to-Sea Trail to the Linville River.

CAMBRIC BRANCH TRAIL

Length: 1.3 miles one way
Difficulty: very strenuous
Elevation change: 1,500 feet
USGS quadrant: Ashford
Access: This trail can only be reached from the Shortoff
  Mountain Trail 2.3 miles south of the Table Rock
  Parking Area (N 35° 51' 36", W 81° 52' 50"). See
  maps on pages 122–123.

This is one of the most brutal, remote, primitive, and unflinchingly steep trails in the entire national forest. It descends to one of the more pristine and least-visited corners of Linville Gorge.

From the fork in the Shortoff Mountain Trail, the Cambric Branch Trail passes a small campsite after 10 yards, then descends to a second campsite in a saddle. At 0.4 mile, you will crest a small knob that offers incredible views to the south of Shortoff Mountain. From here, the trail makes a sharp right by a pitch pine and rapidly descends the spine of the ridge for nearly 1 mile. The last 100 yards of the trail are nearly vertical; they constitute more of a climb (or a fall) than a hike. When you reach the bottom, you will enter a ravine where there is often standing water. On the other side of the berm is a campsite beneath a large beech beside the river (N 51' 14", W 53' 56"). Directly across the river, a piece of pink tape hangs on a rhododendron. There is a nice series of rapids 100 yards upstream. It is a beautiful 0.25-mile hike downstream through a hickory grove and old-growth hemlock to the confluence of Cambric Branch and the Linville River. There are several large boulders in the river 100 yards downstream. There is no easy place to cross the river here. If you must cross, you can expect to wade.

If you are coming from the Linville Gorge Trail, the Cambric Branch Trail is difficult to find. Your best bet is to find the campsite beneath the large beech, go east past the berm and the ravine, veer to the left, and begin the steep climb to the left of a white oak, a hickory, and a hemlock with mossy trunks that are tightly grouped.

Very few loops are available on the East Rim of Linville Gorge. There is one rather remote and strenuous option, however.

EAST RIM LOOP
Length: 3.2 miles
Difficulty: strenuous
Elevation change: 1,050 feet
USGS quadrant: Linville Falls

Begin the Table Rock Gap Trail at its trailhead beside Spence Ridge and follow it until it ends on the Table Rock Summit Trail. Turn right on the Table Rock Summit Trail, then turn right on the Little Table Rock Trail and follow it until it ends on the Spence Ridge Trail. Turn right on the Spence Ridge Trail to return to the starting point.

HARPER CREEK AREA

The Wilson Creek Area is a proposed wilderness area located in Avery, Burke, and Caldwell Counties. The state legislature has not yet decided whether to provide this spectacular, rugged section of Pisgah National Forest with the same special protection afforded the Linville Gorge and Shining Rock Wilderness Areas. The dozens of trails in the Wilson Creek Area penetrate various remote coves and scenic ridges and provide nearly 100 miles of unparalleled hiking splendor.

Lost Cove Creek, Harper Creek, and Upper Creek are the three major creek basins that flow from the west into Wilson Creek. Each of these basins has its own outstanding trail system. This book, however, focuses on the Harper Creek Basin, which encompasses Harper Creek, North Harper Creek, and Raiders Camp Creek, plus Long Ridge, Persimmon Ridge, and the various cliffs overlooking Lost Cove to the north. These are some of the most pristine trout waters anywhere in Pisgah National Forest, and the steep terrain creates some of the most spectacular waterfalls and swimming holes as well. Not to be

Wilson Creek
PHOTO BY CAROLYN SAKOWSKI

outdone, the remote, dense coves provide protection to a surprisingly diverse array of flora and fauna.

These coves were the site of a few early settlements—notably, Kawana to the west and the larger Mortimer and Edgemont to the east. Mortimer was a major logging community boasting 1,000 residents in the first quarter of the 20th century. Natural disasters—massive fires in 1916 and 1925 and floods in 1916 and 1940—put an end to that. Little is left of the community today. Those interested in learning more and viewing some artifacts from that time are highly encouraged to pay a visit to the charming, old post office in Edgemont—now a small country store—on N.C. 90 almost 2 miles west of S.R. 1328.

Described below are over 20 miles of trails and numerous breathtaking day hikes that range from high, rocky cliff walks to dense, lush creek-hopping. Because this area is so diverse and fragile, and because it is not yet fully protected, it is especially important that hikers and campers make as little impact as possible. These trails are wild, remote, and pristine; let's keep them that way.

Several of the trails begin or end on F.R. 464.

If you are coming from the northwest, take the Blue Ridge Parkway south to Old Jonas Ridge Road, a dirt road on the left (east). At the time of this book's publication, there was no sign for this road. It is located 0.9 mile north of N.C. 181. Drive 1.8 miles down Jonas Ridge Road until you see Long Ridge Baptist Church on the left. At the church, turn left down F.R. 464.

If you are coming from the southwest, take N.C. 181. Turn east (right, if you are coming up the mountain) on to S.R. 1401 (Mortimer Road), located just past a Chevron station on the left. After 2.2 miles on S.R. 1401, turn right on Clarktown Road at Pitman Gap Community Church. Drive 0.5 mile on Clarktown Road to Long Ridge Baptist Church and turn right on to F.R. 464.

If you are coming from the east, take N.C. 181 out of Morganton. About 10 miles north of town, turn right on Brown Mountain Beach Road. Drive 5.2 miles east, then turn left on S.R. 1328 (Winchester or Wilson Creek Roads). After 8.9 miles, turn left on N.C. 90. After 1.8 miles on N.C. 90, you will reach F.R. 464, on the left; it is labeled Pineola Road.

A few of the trails are located on F.R. 58, which branches south off F.R. 464 some 2.6 miles east of Long Ridge Baptist Church and 7 miles west of N.C. 90.

HARPER CREEK TRAIL (#260)

Length: 6.3 miles one way
Difficulty: moderate
Elevation change: 950 feet
USGS quadrant: Chestnut Mountain
Access: The eastern trailhead (N 35° 58' 48", W 81° 45'
    53") is difficult to find. It is on S.R. 1328 some 1.3
    miles south of N.C. 90 and 7.6 miles north of Brown
    Mountain Beach Road. You'll find only a small trail
    sign—and no parking—at the trailhead. The western
    trailhead (N 35° 59' 18", W 81° 49' 29") is located on
    F.R. 58 some 4.3 miles south of F.R. 464. See maps
    on pages 162–163.

The trail begins a moderate climb into a dense cove of dog-
hobble, Christmas fern, rhododendron, holly, Eastern hemlock,
galax, pipsissewa, aster, violets, trillium, wild ginger, thalictrum,
and other early-spring wildflowers. It crests a small ridge at 0.4
mile, where Yellow Buck Trail descends from the right (N 58'
35", W 46' 6"). There is no marker for this junction; look for
green tape on an old pine tree and a wildlife sign just past the
trailhead. From here, the trail descends and ascends through
holly, mountain laurel, and ground cedar high above the creek.
There is an easily missed junction at 1.3 miles (N 58' 42", W 46'
51"). The Harper Creek Trail forks off uphill to the right beside
a trout sign on a pine tree; straight ahead is the beginning of the
Raiders Camp Trail, which passes a large campsite to the left
before crossing Harper Creek shortly thereafter. There is a second fork at 1.6 miles (N 58' 52", W 46' 52"). The Harper Creek
Trail forks off to the right; straight ahead is the access trail to
Harper Creek Falls. (The access trail follows a flat roadbed for
0.1 mile, where a spur trail drops to the left to the base of the

falls. Some ropes are tied to a tree here; you must use them to reach the base of the falls. The spectacular Harper Creek Falls cascades down two 50-foot tiers into a small pool, then drops an additional 10 to 15 feet into a deep pool perhaps 50 feet in diameter.)

Continue to the right on the Harper Creek Trail. You will climb above the falls, then pass a campsite 0.2 mile later. The trail crosses Harper Creek for the first time at 2.4 miles; you'll see blue tape on an alder and a campsite on the other side. Unless the water is low, you will have to wade here. You will cross the creek 0.2 mile later, again 0.2 mile after that, and a fourth time 30 yards after that. You will approach an old signpost marked by a cable and pink tape just before the 3.4-mile mark. Straight ahead begins the North Harper Creek Trail; the Harper Creek Trail descends to the left, hops across a small island, and crosses Harper Creek at its confluence with North Harper Creek. On the other side of the creek are a good campsite and lots of alder. The trail continues alongside the creek for 0.1 mile, then crosses it downstream from an excellent pool. You will cross the creek at 3.7 miles and again 75 yards later. At 4.1 miles, the trail crosses a small tributary flowing in from the north. It then rock-hops across Harper Creek 50 yards later. Less than 0.1 mile later, you will approach one of the best swimming holes anywhere; the creek shelf drops a good six feet, creating a jumping platform into a large, deep pool. The trail crosses the creek 20 yards later and veers to the far right in a spacious flood plain. Sixty yards later, you will cross the creek again. At 4.7 miles, the trail crosses the creek on a particularly large, wide rock downstream from a nice cascade; on the other bank is a carsonite sign noting that

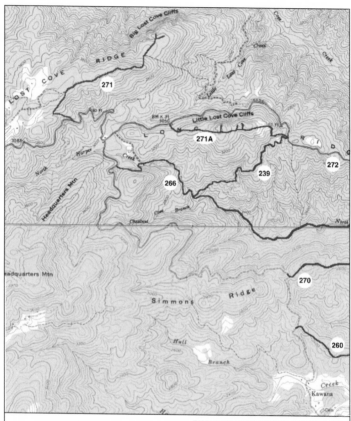

TOPOGRAPHICAL MAP COURTESY OF MAPTECH, INC.

HARPER CREEK AREA

239 North Harper Creek Falls Trail
265 Yellow Buck Trail
266A North Harper Creek Access Trail
270 Persimmon Ridge Trail
271A Little Lost Cove Cliffs Trail
277 Raiders Camp Trail

260 Harper Creek Trail
266 North Harper Creek Trail
268 Greentown Trail
271 Big Lost Cove Cliffs Trail
272 Darkside Cliffs Trail

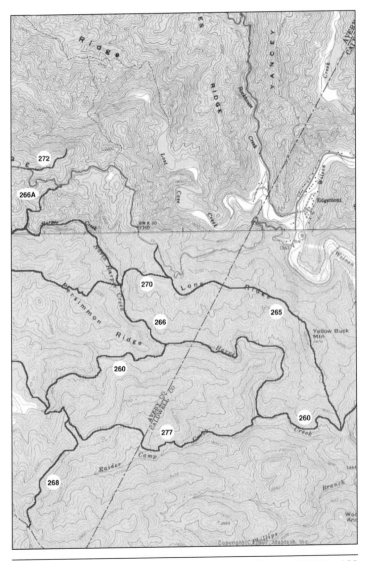

horseback riding is forbidden on this trail. Up ahead is a small campsite. Beyond the campsite, the ascent becomes more moderate. After 100 yards, just before beginning a series of switchbacks, you will be able to see the breathtaking rock amphitheater created by South Harper Creek Falls; the name South Harper Creek Falls is misleading, since there is no South Harper Creek. The trail reaches the top of the waterfall at 5.1 miles. The 200-foot cascade is one of the most scenic waterfalls in the state. While you cannot see much of it from this perspective, the view of the 300-foot cliffs on the opposite side of the bowl is unparalleled. To gain a better view of the waterfall itself, you must hike upstream, turn left on the Raiders Camp Trail, and follow it for almost 0.2 mile to a cliff overlook. The Harper Creek Trail forks about 20 yards past the top of the waterfall. The left fork goes down to the creek and the trailhead for the Raiders Camp Trail; the right fork switches back and begins to climb the ridge beneath a diverse hardwood canopy. The ascent is moderate to strenuous for the first 200 yards but mellows to an easy walk after you pass the "USGS Bearing Trees." (Throughout the national forest you can see trees that have metal plates nailed to them that read "USGS Bearing Trees.") After 5.3 miles, the trail passes a dirt road and a large clearing on private property near the old Kawana settlement. Looking to the southwest, you will see the knob on Ripshin Ridge at 210° and 3.3 miles, Sugar Knob at 248° and 1.5 miles, and Cold Mountain at 67° and 2.8 miles. From here, you will enjoy an easy stroll along the ridge top through a wide-open forest of young white pine, dogwood, holly, sourwood, and mountain laurel. You will come to a fork in the trail at a small campsite at 4.8 miles. The spur trail to the left goes nowhere; the main trail continues to the right and reaches F.R. 58 after 0.5 mile. At the road, it is 0.5 mile to the right to the trailhead for the Persimmon Ridge Trail and 4 miles to the trailhead for the North Harper Creek Trail.

NORTH HARPER CREEK TRAIL (#266)

Length: 4.5 miles one way
Difficulty: moderate to strenuous
Elevation change: 1,400 feet
USGS quadrants: Chestnut Mountain, Grandfather Mountain
Access: To reach the western trailhead, turn south off F.R. 464 on to F.R. 58 some 2.6 miles east of Long Ridge Baptist Church. The trailhead is 0.3 mile down F.R. 58, just past a bend on the left (N 36° 0' 25", W 81° 51' 3"). The eastern trailhead is at the confluence of North Harper Creek and Harper Creek (N 35° 59' 12", W 81° 47' 39"). See maps on pages 162–163.

Even a skilled rock-hopper can expect to get wet on this trail. There are well over a dozen creek crossings, many of which require wading. Except during droughts, the water level is knee deep or higher in some places. Thus, you are encouraged to forgo large, waterproof boots (which you'll spend too much time removing) in favor of river/sport sandals.

The North Harper Creek Trail begins on the northern riverbank at the confluence of North Harper Creek and Harper Creek. The trailhead, surrounded by mountain alder and wild geranium, has a wooden post marked with orange tape. Although the trail is orange blazed, there are few of these blazes at first; rather, there are only the ubiquitous white dots. The trail descends to the first of many creek crossings after 0.2 mile, continues past a campsite, and crosses again 50 yards later. A tenth of a mile later, you will reach two good campsites and make another creek crossing. After 0.75 mile, you will cross the creek again, walk past a campsite and a swimming hole, and reach the junction with the Persimmon Ridge Trail, marked by a single white dot on a narrow tree; this junction can be rather confusing when you are coming from the present direction. The North Harper Creek Trail crosses the creek here; the Persimmon Ridge Trail continues straight ahead before gradually ascending to the left away from the creek. Thus, if you've gone more than 0.8 mile from the trailhead and see that the creek is below to your right, you've inadvertently taken the wrong path. On the other side of the creek are two white dots on a maple and an easily missed, old wooden sign. The Persimmon Ridge Trail forks off to the right and ascends 0.7 mile to F.R. 464; the North Harper Creek Trail continues to the left. Almost 0.1 mile later, you will reach a particularly deep creek crossing. On the other side of the creek, the trail opens up into a wide, flat, sandy grove of yellow birch ringed with campsites. At 1.2 miles, it steepens as it passes a wonderful waterfall that drops nearly 40 feet into a narrow, rocky channel that opens into a superb swimming hole; the climb down to the swimming hole is slippery and steep—and therefore not recommended. For the next 0.3 mile, the creek is dotted with similarly magnificent cascades and swimming holes. At 1.5 miles, you will pass another waterfall and swimming hole, continue through a hemlock grove, and cross the creek. There is a large campsite to the right at 1.8 miles, followed by a smaller one to the right 50 yards later. Soon thereafter, you will enter a stand of young birch trees overenthusiastically blazed orange. To your right, the North Harper Creek Access Trail begins its 1-mile ascent to F.R. 464. A tenth of a mile later, the North Harper Creek Trail comes to another large campsite; look for the designation "266" and an arrow pointing to the right on a tulip poplar. Just beyond the campsite, it crosses the creek again; you'll see orange and yellow tape on both sides of creek. There is a small campsite on the other side. You will then continue beneath a thicket of holly and rhododendron lined with club moss, passing to the left of the creek for 0.2 mile before crossing it again. At 2.2 miles, you will reach a campsite marked by an arrow on an old tulip poplar. Just past the campsite, the trail crosses the creek again. You will cross again 100 yards later and pass alongside an entire hillside of lady fern. Two tenths of a mile after that, you will reach a large campsite and yet another tulip tree with an arrow and "266" painted on it. The trail crosses the creek 0.2 mile later, and again 0.1 mile after that. At 2.8 miles, it passes a small campsite and begins a moderate ascent. The steepening topography has created a long series of small, noisy cascades, each of which empties into a quiet pool that is well suited for swimming or fishing. Along the way, you will find lots of Clinton's lily and the perfectly named fairy wand. The North Harper Creek Falls Trail ascends to the right at 3.3 miles (N 0' 12", W 50' 23"). This junction is difficult to spot; the once-red blazes are now a faded pink, and the old ax mark on a tulip poplar is largely overgrown. The only sure way to find the trail is to continue ahead toward Chestnut Cove Branch Falls, then backtrack several yards until you see the blaze. Just past the junction you will see Chestnut Cove Branch Falls, an attractive waterfall that slides almost 175 feet to a pool at the base. The waterfall is actually on North Harper Creek, rather than Chestnut Cove Branch; it is named after that latter branch, however, because the two creeks join just above the falls and because of the nearby North Harper Creek Falls. About 50 yards past the waterfall, the trail reaches North Harper Creek. Turn to the right and continue upstream for five or 10 yards before crossing. On the other side of the creek, you will pass a campsite before reaching the spectacular North Harper Creek Falls, where the water rushes off a drop nearly 40 feet high into a small, deep pool. Though you can't tell from this perspective, there is a second waterfall just above that slides several hundred feet down before creating this one. To the left of the waterfall, the trail begins a strenuous ascent. A hundred yards later, it switches back sharply to the right; look for the orange tape on an old stump. Straight ahead, an old, abandoned trail continues into Chestnut Cove. A tenth of a mile later, the trail crosses the creek at the top of North Harper Creek Falls. Fifty yards later, you will cross the creek again; you'll see a piece of orange tape on a rhododendron branch. On the other side, you'll make a sharp right and continue an easy-to-moderate ascent alongside the creek through witch hazel and rhododendron. A tenth of a mile later, the trail rock-hops the creek and ascends to a nice, large campsite surrounded by black birch, galax, wood aster, and partridgeberry. From here, you'll make a moderate-to-strenuous ascent on a narrow, old roadbed, passing some rock formations and boisterous cascades along the way. The trail reaches a large, tricky rock exposure at 4.2 miles (N 0' 25", W 50' 49"); look for a piece of orange tape on a mountain laurel. Up the hill to the right, you'll see a private cabin. From here, you'll continue straight ahead across the rockface; the trail to your right leads to private property. Fifty yards later, you'll cross the creek; you'll see a red dot on a hemlock and a wooden sign reading, "North Harper Creek—Artificial Lures Only." At 4.5 miles, the trail ends on F.R. 58.

PERSIMMON RIDGE TRAIL (#270)

Length: 3 miles
Difficulty: moderate
Elevation change: 975 feet
USGS quadrant: Chestnut Mountain
Access: The western trailhead is on F.R. 58 some 3.8 miles south of F.R. 464 (N 35° 59' 41", W 81° 49' 33"). The eastern trailhead is on F.R. 464 some 7.3 miles east of Long Ridge Baptist Church and 2.3 miles west of N.C. 90 (N 59' 53", W 47' 42"). See maps on pages 162–163.

From the western trailhead on F.R. 58, the trail starts a moderate ascent on a wide path atop the ridge, passing beneath a mixture of white and chestnut oak, mountain laurel, rhododendron, Carolina silverbell, sourwood, and—naturally—persimmon. You will crest a small knob at 0.2 mile and begin a short moderate-to-strenuous descent to a saddle. For the next mile, the trail follows a series of easy-to-moderate undulations along the open forest of the ridge top. It begins a strenuous descent after 1.4 miles and reaches North Harper Creek and the junction with the North Harper Creek Trail at 2 miles (N 59' 38", W 48' 2"). To your right, the North Harper Creek Trail heads east for 0.7 mile to its junction with the Harper Creek Trail. The Persimmon Ridge Trail and the North Harper Creek Trail both cross the creek here. On the other side, the Persimmon

Ridge Trail forks right and begins a moderate-to-strenuous climb through hemlock, dog-hobble, and rhododendron. After 0.3 mile, it briefly follows a small spring upstream to its ground source. The trail mellows to an easy-to-moderate ascent through a broad, open hardwood forest. You will come to a T intersection with an old roadbed at 2.6 miles (N 59' 41", W 47' 37"). Here, you'll find a large campsite, a brown signpost with "PR" painted on it, two roadbeds to the right, and one roadbed to the left. Of the two roadbeds to the right, the one farther to the right is a deceptive trail that leads nowhere; the one to the left is the Yellow Buck Trail, which heads 2.4 miles to the Harper Creek Trail. The roadbed to the left leads 0.3 mile to F.R. 464, where the trail ends.

YELLOW BUCK TRAIL (#265)

Length: 2.7 miles one way
Difficulty: strenuous for the first 0.7 mile, easy to
    moderate thereafter
Elevation change: 780 feet
USGS quadrant: Chestnut Mountain
Access: The southeastern trailhead is located on the
    Harper Creek Trail 0.4 mile west of S.R. 1328 (N 58'
    35", W 46' 6"). The northwestern trailhead is on F.R.
    464 some 7.3 miles east of Long Ridge Baptist
    Church and 2.3 miles west of N.C. 90. The
    Persimmon Ridge Trail begins at the same trailhead (N
    59' 53", W 47' 42"). See maps on pages 162–163.

The orange-blazed trail immediately begins a strenuous ascent of an old roadbed; the grade becomes increasingly steep as you climb. You'll have a brief respite from the otherwise brutal ascent after 0.5 mile as you crest a small knob and drop to a saddle. The trail reaches the summit of Yellow Buck Mountain at 0.9 mile. There is a small campsite at the top. In the winter months, you will enjoy an outstanding, panoramic view here. To the west is Harper Creek Valley, where Chestnut Mountain is visible at 233° and 2.6 miles and Headquarters Mountain at 279° and 5.3 miles. Grandfather Mountain is to the north at 351° and 8.9 miles. The Wilson Creek Valley is to the east; you'll see Rocky Knob at 47° and 9.2 miles. From the summit, the trail descends steeply for 0.2 mile to a saddle. Thereafter, it follows a series of easy-to-moderate undulations among white pine, holly, mountain laurel, and blueberry. The trail comes to a campsite and a major intersection at 2.4 miles. Immediately behind and to the left is an old roadbed that leads nowhere; at the far left, a brown post with "PR" carved into it marks the junction with the Persimmon Ridge Trail; and straight ahead is a wide, old roadbed that leads to F.R. 464 after 0.3 mile.

RAIDERS CAMP TRAIL (#277)

Length: 2.6 miles one way
Difficulty: moderate
Elevation change: 900 feet
USGS quadrant: Chestnut Mountain
Access: The trail begins and ends on the Harper Creek Trail. The western trailhead is located at the top of South Harper Creek Falls (N 35° 58' 47", W 81° 48' 40"). The eastern trailhead is on the eastern bank of Harper Creek just north of its confluence with Raiders Camp Creek (N 35° 58' 42", W 81° 46' 50"). See maps on pages 162–163.

The western trailhead is at a fork in the Harper Creek Trail just above South Harper Creek Falls. The Raiders Camp Trail forks down to the left and follows the creek 30 yards upstream before crossing it at a safe point. On the other side of the creek, the trail switches back a couple of times and begins a moderate ascent. A tenth of a mile later, it passes a small spur trail to the left; the spur trail descends to spectacular views of South Harper Creek Falls. You will switch back to the right a few more times before reaching a roadbed after 0.3 mile. To your right is the terminus of the Greentown Trail, which goes 1.3 miles to F.R. 198; the Raiders Camp Trail follows the roadbed to the left. From here, it is an easy stroll beneath hemlock and rhododendron along a wide path that follows the ridge contour into a bowl-shaped cove. From the cove, you'll have an excellent view of Grandfather Mountain to the north. You will reach a small clearing at 0.9 mile (N 58' 40", W 48' 4"). The old roadbed behind and to the right goes east to a junction with the Greentown Trail; the main trail continues straight ahead, past a tulip poplar marked with orange tape. From here, the trail begins a moderate descent on the roadbed through a serene grove of young tulip poplar. Almost 0.9 mile later, it briefly approaches Raiders Camp Creek, where you'll see a spectacular small waterfall and a swimming hole to the right. The trail then veers left away from the water. It approaches an excellent, large campsite to ·the right by the creek at 2.3 miles. Fifty yards later, you'll reach a second large campsite to the right; the painted orange arrow indicates the creek, not the trail. The trail makes an easy descent alongside the creek for the next 0.3 mile, at which point Raiders Camp Creek flows into Harper Creek. A small campsite is located here; you'll see an old railroad tie and "Harper" painted on an old hemlock. The trail makes a sharp left, heads upstream, and crosses Harper Creek at an island in the water; look for an orange arrow and a white dot on a boulder. On the other side of Harper Creek are plenty of orange blazes. The trail continues perpendicularly away from the creek. After 50 yards, it passes a large campsite to the right. A hundred yards later, it ends at the junction with the Harper Creek Trail. The Harper Creek Trail goes straight ahead for 1.3 mile to S.R. 1328. It then forks up and to the left to the beginning of the Raiders Camp Trail at South Harper Creek Falls at 3.8 miles and to F.R. 58 at 5 miles.

GREENTOWN TRAIL (#268)

Length: 1.3 miles one way
Difficulty: moderate
Elevation change: 400 feet
USGS quadrant: Chestnut Mountain
Access: Turn off N.C. 181 on to F.R. 982 some 4.9 miles north of the junction with Brown Mountain Beach Road. There is no sign for F.R. 982; there is only a small, paved turnout on the east (the right, if you are coming up from Morganton) that quickly turns into a descending dirt road. Drive 4.3 miles down F.R. 982 to F.R. 198 and turn left. You will definitely need a four-wheel-drive vehicle for F.R. 198, which ends at a cul-de-sac after 3.5 miles. An old roadbed forks off to the left; the trailhead is located to the right (N 35° 57' 58", W 81° 48' 52"). See maps on pages 162–163.

The white-blazed trail makes a moderate descent on a wide, washed-out roadbed. After 0.1 mile, it forks to the right at a carsonite sign. You will reach a second trail junction at 0.9 mile (N 58' 33", W 48' 26"). The road bends around to the right; the carsonite sign to the left indicates that the Mountains-to-Sea Trail forks off to the left. Two tenths of a mile later, you will come to a T intersection, marked by a piece of black tape on a young red oak. The trail to the left leads toward private property; the main trail continues to the right. A hundred yards later, the road bends to the right and the Greentown Trail ends at an intersection with the Raiders Camp Trail (N 35° 58' 42", W 81° 48' 31"). To the left, it is 0.3 mile to South Harper Creek Falls and the junction with the Harper Creek Trail; to the right, it is 2.2 miles to Harper Creek and the junction with the Harper Creek Trail.

NORTH HARPER CREEK FALLS TRAIL (#239)

Length: 1.3 miles one way
Difficulty: easy for the first mile, moderate to strenuous at the end
Elevation change: 400 feet
USGS quadrant: Grandfather Mountain
Access: The trailhead is located on F.R. 464 some 4.6 miles from Long Ridge Baptist Church and 5 miles from the junction with N.C. 90. There is a wooden sign here that incorrectly identifies the trail as "North Harper Creek Trail, #238." To the right of the sign is a metal gate, behind which is the Little Lost Cove Cliffs Trail (N 36° 0' 37", W 81° 49' 33"). See maps on pages 162–163. See maps on pages 162–163.

The trail begins on an old roadbed and gradually descends into the valley through lots of dogwood, sourwood, tulip polar, white pine, red maple, umbrella magnolia, and Dutchman's-pipe. You'll reach a large campsite to the left after 0.2 mile and a small spring 0.1 mile beyond that. The trail crosses a stream on a wooden bridge at 0.6 mile and then wraps around to the left, passing through a young grove of tulip poplar before beginning an easy-to-moderate descent. After 1 mile, you'll see an orange arrow on a red oak that marks a fork in the trail. The roadbed continues straight ahead; the North Harper Creek Trail forks off to the right. A hundred yards later, the trail forks to the left; look for the pink tape on a mountain laurel. It makes a strenuous descent for the 0.1 mile before ending at the top of Chestnut Cove Branch Falls. To the left, the North Harper Creek Trail descends toward Harper Creek; to the right, the North Harper Creek Trail ascends for 0.1 mile to the fabulous North Harper Creek Falls.

NORTH HARPER CREEK ACCESS TRAIL (#266A)

Length: 1 mile one way
Difficulty: easy
Elevation change: 350 feet
USGS quadrant: Grandfather Mountain
Access: The trailhead is on F.R. 464 some 5.9 miles from Long Ridge Baptist Church and 3.7 miles from N.C. 90. To the right is a small pull-off area with a campsite and a trail sign (N 36° 0' 19", W 81° 48' 30"). See maps on pages 162–163.

This trail is popular with those who like to fly-fish, as it provides a relatively short, easy access to one of the region's best trout streams. The orange-blazed trail begins with an easy descent beneath white pine, Eastern hemlock, and mountain laurel. You will cross a small stream after 0.2 mile. The trail crosses a small ridge line and makes a sharp bend to the right at 0.4 mile. Two tenths of a mile later, you will cross a second stream among lots of striped maple, lady fern, and anemone. At 0.8 mile, a small footpath descends steeply to the left toward a large campsite; please do not use this path, as it severely erodes the hillside. A second trail 0.1 mile later also leads to the campsite. After 0.9 mile, the North Harper Creek Access Trail ends amidst a flurry of young birch trees heavily blazed with orange paint. To the left, the North Harper Creek Trail continues 1.8 miles to its junction with the Harper Creek Trail; to the right, it is 1.5 miles to Chestnut Cove Branch Falls, 1.6 miles to North Harper Creek Falls, and 2.7 miles to F.R. 58.

Three separate, unconnected trails overlook Lost Cove. Each trail offers spectacular views of Grandfather Mountain, Lost Cove, and the Wilson Creek Valley.

BIG LOST COVE CLIFFS TRAIL (#271)

Length: 1.5 miles one way
Difficulty: easy to moderate
Elevation change: 320 feet
USGS quadrangle: Grandfather Mountain
Access: From Long Ridge Baptist Church, turn down F.R. 464 and drive 1.6 miles to the parking area on the right. The trailhead, located on the left, is marked (N 36° 00' 43", W 81° 51' 27"). See maps on pages 162–163.

Note: At the time of this book's publication, the Forest Service had closed access to the cliffs, so as not to disturb the nests of reintroduced peregrine falcons. Those interested in seeing the cliffs should skip this trail and hike the not-to-be-outdone Little Lost Cove Cliffs Trail instead.

The Big Lost Cove Cliffs Trail begins a moderate climb along a wide, eroded path beneath lots of rhododendron, mountain laurel, hemlock, and pine. The trail comes to a T intersection at 0.3 mile; an old roadbed comes in from the left and the main trail veers off to the right (N 0' 56", W 51' 31"). Note: This intersection is easily missed on the return route, so remember it well. Past the junction, the ascent becomes easy. A small trail marked by a cairn jumps off to the right after 0.5 mile; this spur trail peters out after 0.1 mile but offers a decent view of Simmons Ridge to the south. After 0.9 mile, you will reach a good campsite and a fire ring among lots of galax, crested dwarf iris, halberd-leaved violets, and blueberry (N 1' 4", W 51' 7"). The trail crests a ridge at 1.1 miles, then continues down to the right; ahead and to the left is a small scramble trail (N 1' 6", W 50' 55"). A tenth of a mile later, you will reach a fork in the trail; continue to the right. There is a major trail junction at 1.3 miles, marked by a large stone in the trail with a white arrow painted on it. The trail coming in from the left is the left fork from the last junction; the trail to the right descends to Little Lost Cove Creek (N 1' 10", W 50' 49"). A hundred yards past the next large campsite, you will reach another trail junction (N 1' 18", W 50' 42"). If you veer to the left, it is 0.1 mile to the cliffs (N 1' 20", W 50' 43"). If you take the path to the right, you'll walk past a large campsite completely stripped of firewood. A tenth of a mile beyond the campsite is another trail junction (N 1' 19", W 50' 39"). The small trail to the left leads to a rock outcropping; the trail straight ahead leads to a another cliff (N 1' 19", W 50' 38"). From any vantage point on the cliff, Grandfather Mountain is directly in front of you. The stream that begins to the far left and flows eastward is Lost Cove Creek, which eventually joins Rockhouse Creek just past Hughs Ridge to form Wilson Creek.

LITTLE LOST COVE CLIFFS TRAIL (#271A)

Length: 1.2 miles one way
Difficulty: moderate
Elevation change: 380 feet
USGS quadrangle: Grandfather Mountain
Access: From Long Ridge Baptist Church, turn on to F.R. 464 and continue straight ahead past F.R. 58, The trailhead, marked by a sign, is on the right at 3.2 miles. Parking is available on either side of the road (N 36° 0' 42", W 81° 50' 36"). See maps on pages 162–163.

The trail makes a moderate-to-strenuous ascent along an eroded path lined with rhododendron, galax, mountain laurel, ground cedar, and hemlock. It reaches the ridge line at 0.2 mile, after which the ascent is easy to moderate for the next 0.2 mile. The first of three spur trails begins to the left at 0.4 mile; a large boulder in the trail marks the intersection (N 0' 39", W 50' 9"). This trail heads north for 0.1 mile to the highest point along the Little Lost Cove Cliffs Trail (N 0' 42", W 50' 9") and provides truly incredible views of Grandfather Mountain and Lost Cove. The main trail continues straight ahead and descends gradually for 0.1 mile to a nice campsite in a ridge saddle (N 0' 40", W 50' 1"). Just past the campsite, the second cliff trail breaks off to the left. This narrow path reaches the cliffs after 100 yards and offers an astounding vista (N 0' 43", W 50' 0"). A tenth of a mile beyond this junction, the third spur trail breaks off to the left. It goes 100 yards to yet another amazing overlook (N 0' 43", W 49' 57"). Notice the spring beauty, purple-crested dwarf iris, violets, mountain laurel, and flame azalea along the way. At 0.8 mile, you will descend into a bucolic meadow, where you'll see some old apple trees and tons of meadow parsnip. There are no good views from the northern side of the meadow, but the southern side offers a nice view of the Harper Creek Valley. The trail goes across the meadow and down to an old roadbed. From here, it is recommended that you follow the old road to the right, rather than trying to find the old, steep footpath directly across. Along the road, you'll see lots of mountain mint and Clinton's lily. The two paths reconnect after 0.25 mile. The trail ends a little more than 0.1 mile later at a gate on F.R. 464 (N 0' 38", W 49' 33"). Downhill to the right is the trailhead for the North Harper Creek Falls Trail; directly across the road is a footpath that goes nowhere. The trailhead is 1.4 mile to the left on F.R. 464. You can either backtrack, return to the trailhead via F.R. 464, or venture down the North Harper Creek Falls Trail and turn right on to the North Harper Creek Trail for a *highly* recommended 4.2-mile loop.

DARKSIDE CLIFFS TRAIL (#272)

Length: 0.5 mile one way
Difficulty: easy
Elevation change: 300 feet
USGS quadrangle: Grandfather Mountain
Access: Turn on to F.R. 464 at Long Ridge Baptist Church
and drive 5.2 miles to the grassy parking area on
the right. A small trail begins on the left (N 36° 0' 28",
W 81° 48' 55"). Since there is no sign for the
trailhead, the trail is easily missed. See maps on
pages 162–163.

Note the abundance of star grass at the trailhead. You will begin an easy walk on a narrow ridge-line trail lined by galax and crested dwarf iris beneath a canopy of mixed hardwoods. After 0.1 mile, the trail reaches the ridge crest. A tenth of a mile after that, it descends into a saddle and turns left (N 0' 28", W 48' 39"); do not take the old footpath directly in front. A quarter-mile later, the trail reaches the cliffs (N 00' 35", W 48' 31"). From the overlook, you will enjoy outstanding views of Lost Cove beginning to the west. Directly across is Timber Ridge. The exposed rockface behind Timber Ridge at 358° and 6.4 miles is the backside of Grandfather Mountain. To the northeast and stretching to the south are Hughs Ridge and Yancey Ridge; between them lies Rockhouse Creek, which flows into Lost Cove Creek. At 110° and 2 miles is the old hamlet of Edgemont, located just north of the confluence of Lost Cove Creek and Wilson Creek.

There are numerous loop options in the Harper Creek area. Since all the trails here are excellent, all the loops are, too. Below are four of the best.

HARPER CREEK LOOP #1
Length: 4.6 miles round trip
Difficulty: moderate with some strenuous sections
Elevation change: 800 feet
USGS quadrants: Grandfather Mountain, Chestnut Mountain

This half-day loop offers outstanding views of Little Lost Cove Cliffs, Chestnut Cove Branch Falls, and North Harper Creek Falls. It begins with the Little Lost Cove Cliffs Trail. At the end of that trail, turn right and descend on the North Harper Creek Falls Trail. When you reach the end of the trail at Chestnut Cove Branch Falls, turn right on the North Harper Creek Trail and follow it to its end on F.R. 58. Walk up the road 0.3 mile to F.R. 464, then turn right to return to the Little Lost Cove Cliffs Trail 0.6 mile later.

HARPER CREEK LOOP #2
Length: 9 miles round trip
Difficulty: moderate
Elevation change: 875 feet
USGS quadrant: Chestnut Mountain

This full-day option focuses on Harper Creek and Raiders Camp Creek. The loop begins on S.R. 1328 at the trailhead for the Harper Creek Trail. At the top of South Harper Creek Falls at 5.1 miles, turn left on the Raiders Camp Trail. Follow it 2.6 miles back down to its junction with the Harper Creek Trail. From there, backtrack 1.3 miles to the beginning of the loop.

HARPER CREEK LOOP #3

Length: 6.2 miles round trip
Difficulty: moderate with some strenuous sections
Elevation change: 985 feet
USGS quadrant: Chestnut Mountain

This loop combines the pleasant ridge walk of the Persimmon Ridge Trail with a section of the Harper Creek Trail that includes South Harper Creek Falls. From the trailhead on F.R. 58, take the Persimmon Ridge Trail down to the junction with the North Harper Creek Trail at 2 miles. Turn right on the North Harper Creek Trail. Three-quarters of a mile later, turn right on the Harper Creek Trail. Follow it 2.9 miles back to F.R. 58. From there, the starting point is 0.5 mile to the right.

HARPER CREEK LOOP #4

Length: 11.5 miles
Difficulty: strenuous
Elevation change: 1,200 feet
USGS quadrant: Chestnut Mountain

This full-day loop offers the most sustained tour of all Harper Creek's glory. It encompasses Harper Creek and South Harper Creek Falls, Yellow Buck Mountain, Persimmon Ridge, and more. From the trailhead on F.R. 58, follow the Persimmon Ridge Trail for 2.7 miles to the junction with the Yellow Buck Trail. Turn right on the Yellow Buck Trail and follow it for 2.4 miles until it ends on the Harper Creek Trail. Turn right and hike the Harper Creek Trail for 5.9 miles to its end on F.R. 58. From there, the starting point is 0.5 mile to the right.

Poison Ivy, Poison Oak, and Poison Sumac

Poison ivy, poison oak, and poison sumac are common weeds that cause allergic reactions in millions of Americans each year.

Poison ivy grows as a climbing vine or as a nonclimbing shrub. It has three shiny, pointed leaves with serrated edges and produces small, greenish flowers followed by fruits from May to July. Poison ivy grows all along the East Coast and in the Midwest.

Poison oak has three shiny leaves and deeper serrations and has fine hairs on its trunk and leaves. It grows as a shrub in the sandy soil of the Southeast. In the West, it can grow as a shrub or as a climbing vine.

Poison sumac is a shrub characterized by two rows of seven to 13 shiny leaflets. It grows in the peat bogs of the Northeast and the Midwest and in swampy areas in the Southeast.

These weeds are most potent in the spring and summer, when they produce their highest quantity of oil and when the greatest number of people are outside. All three plants are coated with a sticky, oily chemical known as urushiol, which is released when the plant is cut or crushed. Upon exposure to air, urushiol can turn dark brown, which makes it easier to spot. Contact can occur directly by touching the plants or indirectly by touching equipment or the fur of an animal that is carrying the oil. Urushiol is also found in the ashes and smoke of burning plants.

Eighty-five percent of the population will develop an allergic reaction when exposed to these poisonous weeds. The sensitivity usually develops after several exposures. Approximately 10 percent of the population will have a severe reaction, and 10 to 15 percent will have no reaction. Sensitivity tends to decline with age.

The symptoms of exposure to poison ivy, poison oak, and poison sumac are delayed. Usually within 12 to 48 hours, a linear rash appears where the oil first contacted the skin. Redness, swelling, blisters, *continued* and severe itching follow. The blisters eventually crust over. Healing occurs within 10 days. More severe reactions include fever, swelling of the throat and eyes or the entire body, nausea, vomiting, and diarrhea. The rash is not contagious and does not spread, though it may seem to break out in new areas later. This may be because the oil is absorbed less quickly in areas of thicker skin or because the late-affected area received a lower concentration of oil.

Treatment involves washing all exposed areas with soap and water as soon as possible. Urushiol begins to be absorbed within minutes. Those who suspect they have been in contact with the plants should wash their clothing and contaminated gear with detergent and hot water.

Victims can relieve the intense itching with cool showers or oatmeal baths and over-the-counter preparations such as calamine lotion and Burrow's aluminum acetate solution. Over-the-counter hydrocortisone creams are generally not strong enough to be of benefit. However, prescription-strength corticosteroid creams or even oral corticosteroids may be necessary if the rash involves the face, mouth, eyes, or genitals. Oral steroids must be used for at least five days or the rash and swelling may rebound. Victims should not use both oral or topical antihistamines, as toxicity may occur. Frequent scratching can lead to a complication: fingernails can carry bacteria that "superinfect" the afflicted skin. In such cases, the lesions will contain pus, and antibiotics are warranted.

There are new barrier creams that may soon be marketed in the United States. These creams may offer protection by preventing urushiol from penetrating the skin.

At present, follow these measures: wear long-sleeved shirts and pants ; wash exposed skin with soap and water within five to 10 minutes of contact; wash clothes and equipment with detergent in hot water; wear gloves when bathing pets that have been in contact with the plants; know how to recognize and avoid the plants.

OTHER TRAILS IN THE GRANDFATHER RANGER DISTRICT

WOODS MOUNTAIN TRAIL (#218)
Length: 6 miles one way
Difficulty: moderate
Elevation change: 650 feet
USGS quadrants: Celo, Little Switzerland
Access: Make your way to the parking area on the eastern side of the intersection of N.C. 80 and the Blue Ridge Parkway. The trail begins beside a concrete post on an old, overgrown roadbed that parallels the parkway; there is no trail sign (N 35° 46' 13", W 82° 09' 51").

This ridge trail passes through some remarkably diverse flora; nonetheless, it is just as enjoyable in the cold months, when the foliage cannot obstruct the incredible views of Lake Tahoma to the south, the Black Mountains to the west, and Linville Gorge to the east. The Woods Mountain Trail is part of the Mountains-to-Sea Trail, so it is blazed with the ubiquitous white dots.

The trail follows the roadbed past a carsonite "No Motor Vehicles" sign and through lots of spiderwort, fire pink, forget-me-not, rhododendron, mountain laurel, and flame azalea. After

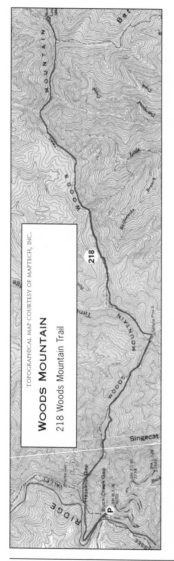

TOPOGRAPHICAL MAP COURTESY OF MAPTECH, INC.

WOODS MOUNTAIN

218 Woods Mountain Trail

0.6 mile, you will reach Hazelnut Gap, where the trail crosses a gate and bends to the left. Almost 100 yards later, it leaves the roadbed and forks to the right (N 46' 22", W 09' 47"). Technically, the trail that followed the roadbed is the Woods Mountain Access Trail, and the actual Woods Mountain Trail begins here; however, this book will treat them as one trail, so all distances are calculated from the parking area.

The trail continues east along the ridge side for 0.25 mile, then reaches the ridge line, where you'll have excellent views to the south of Mackey Mountain and the headwaters of Buck Creek; along the way, you'll pass sundrops, columbine, Solomon's-seal, blueberry, rhododendron, mountain laurel, white pine, locust, chinkapin, oak fern, turkey beard, galax, sweet-fern, bush pea, wood betony, foamflower, and whorled loosestrife beneath a diverse mixture of hardwoods.

Old casino building at Lake Tahoma in McDowell County

An old trail forks to the left at 1.2 mile; a yellow sign notes that this trail is closed due to endangered species protection (N 46" 14", W 09' 15"). A tenth of a mile later, another trail forks to the left and descends to the headwaters of Armstrong Creek. The Woods Mountain Trail continues its easy-to-moderate ascent along the southwestern side of the ridge to a small saddle at 2 miles, then begins a moderate ascent to a small, grassy knob at 2.5 miles (N 45' 54", W 08' 12"). Here, a spur trail descends to the right, while the main trail turns sharply to the left. *Remember this spot well*, as it is easy to miss this turn during the return trip and continue straight down Haines Eyebrow Ridge. There is a fork in the trail at 2.9 miles (N 46' 10", W 07' 54"). To the left, an old trail descends along Timber Ridge to Bad Fork. Half a mile later, at 3.4 miles, you will descend to a small saddle with a decent campsite and a trail junction (N 46' 15", W 07' 30"). To the right, an old logging road descends to Rattlesnake Branch. Another trail forks off to the right at 4.8 miles and descends to Little Buck Creek (N 46' 42", W 06' 18"); straight ahead, the Woods Mountain Trail begins a series of strenuous switch-backs. It crests a knob almost 0.4 mile later at a flat spot beneath a large Eastern hemlock (N 46' 39", W 05' 59"). At 5.8 miles, you will descend to an old roadbed marked by a Mountains-to-Sea Trail carsonite sign (N 47' 38", W 05' 28"). To the right, the logging road descends along Betsy Hensley Ridge to Firescald Creek and eventually Little Buck Creek; to the left, the trail descends briefly before ascending toward the Woods Mountain summit. Two tenths of a mile past the junction, the trail forks. Both forks go to the former site of the Woods Mountain Lookout Tower, where nothing more than four concrete footings remain today (N 46' 41", W 05' 17"). From the summit, on a clear day when the leaves are off the trees, you can see Mackey Mountain at 218° and 5.8 miles. You can also see beyond Open Ridge to Mount Mitchell and the Black Mountains at 269° and 10 miles, Woodys Knob behind the Blue Ridge Parkway at 358° and 7.1 miles, Yellow Mountain at 11° and

A fly fisherman wets a line in Curtis Creek

14.6 miles, Hawksbill at 56° and 14.7 miles, Table Rock at 61° and 13.9 miles, Shortoff Mountain at 76° and 11 miles, and Lake Tahoma at 182° and 3.6 miles.

HICKORY BRANCH TRAIL (#213)

Length: 2 miles one way
Difficulty: easy to moderate to the falls, moderate thereafter
Elevation change: 1,350 feet
USGS quadrangle: Old Fort
Access: From Old Fort, head east on U.S. 70 for 2.2 miles, then turn north (left) on Curtis Creek Road and drive about 5.8 miles to the campground. The trailhead is on the right just past the bridge, 20 yards from the road. It is marked by a carsonite sign (N 35° 41' 25", W 82° 11' 45").

At the trailhead, take the switchback to the left, rather than attempting to scramble straight up the dirt embankment. The trail descends along Hickory Branch, crosses over it, and then turns left past several large campsites in a flat valley of hemlock, tulip poplar, holly, rhododendron, foamflower, jewelweed, doll's eye, dog-hobble, and blue cohosh. It continues up the valley to the right of the branch, then crosses it at 0.3 mile. About a tenth of a mile later, it bends to the left, switches back along the hillside, and comes to a small waterfall. At 0.6 mile, the trail reaches the top of the falls, where it crosses Hickory Branch. It then crosses several more times during the next 0.1 mile. Almost 1 mile into the trail, you will reach a second, superior waterfall, which cascades nearly 60 feet over slick, mossy rocks and lots of wood debris (N 41' 36", W 11' 4"). At the top of the second falls, the trail switches back to the left and begins

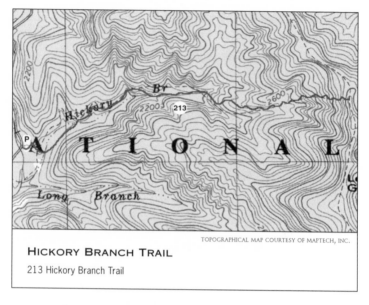

HICKORY BRANCH TRAIL

213 Hickory Branch Trail

a series of moderate switchbacks through blueberry, flame azalea, mountain laurel, chinkapin, and turkey beard. As you ascend away from the water, look back for excellent views over Curtis Creek Valley to Laurel Knob to the west-northwest, Snooks Nose to the west, and Iron Mountain to the west-southwest. The Hickory Branch Trail ends at a **T** intersection along the ridge top at 2 miles (N 41' 41', W 10' 34"). The trail to the left descends to Buckeye Knob; the trail to the right ascends to Lead Mine Gap, then descends to Curtis Creek. However, neither trail is particularly well maintained from this point, so you are best advised to backtrack.

The Cradle of Forestry in America

The Cradle of Forestry in America was established as a National Historic Site by an act of Congress in 1968 to commemorate two landmark events in the history of United States forestry. Those events occurred within the boundaries of what is today the Pisgah Ranger District. Comprising 6,500 acres, the Cradle of Forestry is the site of the beginning of private scientific forest management in the United States and the location of the first technical forestry school in America.

In 1892, George W. Vanderbilt owned over 7,000 acres of land in the area, more than 3,000 of which were in timber. He hired a young, European-trained American forester named Gifford Pinchot to manage his "Biltmore Forest" in the hope of making it a profitable enterprise.

The application of scientific principles to forestry for the purpose of maintaining profitable, renewable forests was new to the United States. It signified a departure from the "cut-and-leave" strategies previously implemented by the lumber industry. The concept of scientific forest management at Biltmore coincided with a conservationist awakening in the United States championed by President Theodore Roosevelt.

The task assigned to Pinchot was formidable. Prior to Vanderbilt's acquisition and consolidation of property near Asheville, the use of the land comprising Biltmore Forest was dictated by the needs of the sustenance farmers who lived there. Timber was cut inefficiently for fuel and fencing and was burned for pasturage. Livestock was allowed to roam freely without regard to the destructive impact of grazing. The land's beauty belied its poor condition as a manageable forest. Efforts at profitability seemed destined to fail. In a report on his first-year efforts, Pinchot noted that it would be many years before Biltmore Forest produced anything more than low-grade
continued

wood suitable only for sale as firewood, cord wood for local brick works, railroad ties, fence posts, lumber, and shingles.

Thus, Pinchot's strategy for improving Biltmore Forest necessarily focused on the future. He planted 1.8 million seedlings of 20 species of trees and hired woods crews to construct roads and other infrastructure. Laborers were paid $1.00 per day, and a mule rented for $.75 per day. Many of the roads and trails in what is now the Pisgah Ranger District were constructed in the effort to make the forest profitable.

Vanderbilt lost interest before Biltmore Forest had a chance to become a profitable undertaking. Nonetheless, the idea of scientific forest management was ahead of its time, as evidenced by its ubiquity in the lumber industry today. Pinchot later became head of the Division of Forestry in the United States Department of Agriculture and a driving force behind the founding of the Yale Forest School.

Technical forestry education in America also has its roots in the Pisgah Ranger District. When Pinchot left Biltmore Forest to pursue other opportunities, Vanderbilt had to look abroad for a replacement. At that time, there were no forestry schools in the United States, and thus no American-trained foresters. Vanderbilt hired Carl Alwin Schenck, a 27-year-old German who had completed a Ph.D. in forestry at the University of Geissen in 1894.

Schenck arrived in North Carolina in the spring of 1895 with very little understanding of the local people and economy but a passion for forestry and an appreciation of the opportunity at hand. He later reflected, "The best fortune I could have met with anywhere became mine in America: fine fields to work in; good health to enjoy; enough to live on; and lots of friendship."

Schenck continued and expanded on Pinchot's plan to make Biltmore Forest profitable, but like Pinchot's, his efforts never achieved profitability. His greater contribution was the founding of the Biltmore Forest School in 1898. Schenck allowed young men to apprentice themselves at Biltmore Forest. In exchange for their unpaid labor, the apprentices were given practical instruction in forestry by Schenck himself. Noting the increasing demand for the apprenticeships and the lack of a technical forestry school in the United States, Schenck formalized his instruction by creating a course catalog, collecting tuition, and offering bachelor of forestry and forest engineer degrees beginning in 1898. Formal forestry education in the United States was born.

In the beginning, the Biltmore Forest School had no trouble recruiting students. Young men from throughout the country applied for a year of instruction to prepare them for careers in the lumber industry or government forest management. Schenck emphasized the necessity of learning forestry in the forest rather than in the classroom. Students heard lectures in the morning before setting out on horseback with Dr. Schenck for an afternoon of hands-on forest work. In the fifteen years that the Biltmore Forest School existed, over 300 students completed the required courses. Many went on to shape the course of American forestry through work in public and private interests.

Unfortunately, George Vanderbilt was more concerned with Schenck's inability to turn a profit than his ability to train foresters, and the two fell out in 1909. In addition, Schenck's philosophy of hands-on forestry training was at odds with the ideas of other prominent foresters, Pinchot included, who favored more rigorous classroom experience at the expense of actual time in the woods. This combination of factors led to the downfall of the first forestry school in America. It was evicted from Biltmore Forest in 1909. After conducting courses in Germany, the Adirondacks, and the American West for

continued

four years, Schenck gave up on his school in 1913.

Today, the Cradle of Forestry National Historic Site offers a visitor center and an interactive exhibition hall. Guests can enjoy a brief movie chronicling the Biltmore Forest story and several exhibitions of both scientific and historic interest. Two guided trails feature historic buildings, a 1915 logging locomotive, an old sawmill, and working craftsmen.

TOECANE

RANGER

DISTRICT

MOUNT MITCHELL STATE PARK

Mount Mitchell State Park, created in 1915, is the oldest state park in North Carolina. The 1,677-acre park extends across much of the Black Mountains and includes the highest peak east of the Rocky Mountains, Mount Mitchell, named after Dr. Elisha Mitchell. The second-highest peak on the ridge, Mount Craig, was named in honor of Governor Locke Craig, who helped establish the state park.

Initially trained in the ministry, Dr. Mitchell soon became a professor of mathematics at the University of North Carolina. He also taught courses in natural history, chemistry, botany, surveying, agriculture, and geology. It was Dr. Mitchell who established that New Hampshire's Mount Washington was not the tallest peak east of the Rockies. Sometime after June 27, 1857, while in the process of collecting measurements to prove that the mountain we now know as Mount Mitchell was taller than the peak now called Clingmans Dome, Dr. Mitchell fell to his death off a small waterfall. That waterfall, now known as Mitchell Falls, is located between Little Piney Ridge and Mitchell Ridge. After a failed search of several days, a famous bear hunter named Big Tom Wilson was called in to assist. He found the body within a day. Big Tom, a peak north of Mount Mitchell, bears his name today. Dr. Mitchell's body was buried at the summit of the highest peak east of the Rockies, which was soon named in his honor.

The state park's trails offer peerless views across the Blue Ridge Mountains. On a clear day, the Great Smoky Mountains are visible to the far west. Mount Mitchell is home to a typical Canadian spruce/fir forest. Mountain ash, false hellebore, white snakeroot, aster, wood sorrel, yellow bead lily, Canadian mayflower, bluets, and St.-John's-wort are among the common species here. Unfortunately, a combination of woolly adelgid infestation and acid rain have depleted or damaged much of the fragile vegetation.

MOUNT MITCHELL SUMMIT TRAIL
Length: 0.2 mile one way
Difficulty: easy to moderate
Elevation change: 120 feet
USGS quadrant: Mount Mitchell
Access: Near Milepost 355 on the Blue Ridge Parkway, located 30 miles northeast of Asheville and 11.2 miles south of N.C. 80, turn north on to S.R. 218 and follow the signs for Mount Mitchell State Park.

From the parking lot, follow the wide gravel path to the left of the visitor center. After 100 yards, the Old Mount Mitchell Trail and the Camp Alice Trail Fork off to the left. A hundred

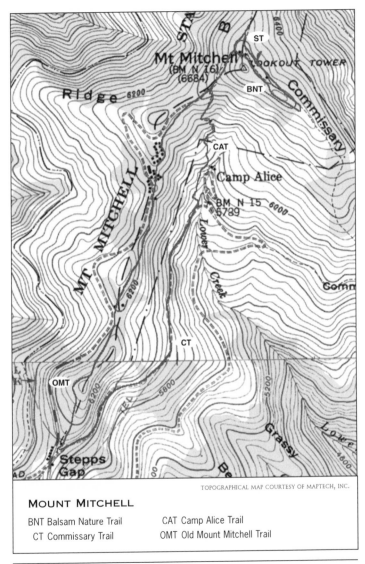

TOPOGRAPHICAL MAP COURTESY OF MAPTECH, INC.

MOUNT MITCHELL

BNT Balsam Nature Trail   CAT Camp Alice Trail
CT Commissary Trail   OMT Old Mount Mitchell Trail

yards later, the Balsam Nature Trail and the Mount Mitchell Trail fork off to the left. Straight ahead, the Mount Mitchell Summit Trail goes to the base of the lookout tower and the tomb of Dr. Elisha Mitchell. Make the short climb to the top of the observation tower to enjoy one of the most rewarding views possible. The large ridge line to the north is the famous, mile-high Black Mountains; Big Tom, Cattail Peak, Deer

Mount Mitchell summit—the highest point in the east

Mountain, and Celo Knob recede into the distance. Beginning to the north, you will see Unaka Mountain at 1° and 25.5 miles, Roan High Knob at 24° and 24.8 miles, Big Yellow Mountain at 34° and 27.3 miles, Yellow Mountain at 42° and 19.3 miles, Grandfather Mountain at 51° and 34.9 miles, Hawksbill at 69° and 23.5 miles, Table Rock at 73° and 23.1 miles, Shortoff Mountain at 82° and 21 miles, Woods Mountain at 89° and 9.9 miles, Mackey Mountain at 125° and 7.8 miles, Green Knob at 149° and 3.9 miles, Pinnacle at 193° and 4.2 miles, Black Mountain at 226° and 40.1 miles, Black Balsam Knob at 233° and 45.6 miles, Mount Pisgah at 234° and 36.2 miles, Cold Mountain at 238° and 41.3 miles, Shining Rock at 235° and 43.3 miles, Richland Balsam at 241° and 49.1 miles, Lickstone Bald at 244° and 46.1 miles, Grassy Bald at 246° and 50.2 miles, Waterrock

Knob at 251° and 53.2 miles, Little Bald Knob on the Cataloochee Divide at 257° and 50.1 miles, Clingmans Dome (the second-highest peak east of the Rockies) at 263° and 70.6 miles, Big Cataloochee Mountain at 267° and 51.5 miles, Mount Le Conte at 268° and 66.2 miles, Mount Sterling at 269° and 48.3 miles, Mount Guyot at 270° and 55.8 miles, Max Patch at 278° and 38.8 miles, Bluff Mountain at 283° and 36.9 miles, Camp Creek Bald at 310° and 30.9 miles, Flattop at 342° and 21.2 miles, and Beauty Spot at 356° and 24.6 miles.

BALSAM NATURE TRAIL

Length: 0.7 mile round trip
Difficulty: easy to moderate
Elevation change: 120 feet
USGS quadrant: Mount Mitchell
Access: Near Milepost 355 on the Blue Ridge Parkway, located 30 miles northeast of Asheville and 11.2 miles south of N.C. 80, turn north on to S.R. 218 and follow the signs for Mount Mitchell State Park. See map on page 199.

The Balsam Nature Trail is a simple, self-guided nature trail that loops through a spruce/fir forest. Along the way, you will see red spruce, Fraser fir, mountain ash, wild raspberry, white snakeroot, aster, false hellebore, bluets, mountain St.-John's-wort, and wood sorrel.

Start by following the Mount Mitchell Summit Trail for a little more than 0.1 mile, then forking off to the left. The Balsam Nature Trail, the Mount Mitchell Trail, and the Mountains-to-Sea Trail run conjunctively for the first 0.3 mile. At marker #11, the Balsam Nature Trail makes a sharp left, while the Mount Mitchell Trail and the Mountains-to-Sea Trail begin a moderate descent to Black Mountain Campground. A spur trail forks down to the right at 0.6 mile. The spur trail descends to the highest spring east of the Rockies; located at an altitude of 6,560 feet, the spring has an average temperature of 36° F. The Balsam Nature Trail continues to left. It ascends for 0.1 mile before returning to the parking lot.

CAMP ALICE TRAIL

Length: 1.1 miles one way
Difficulty: moderate
Elevation change: 650 feet
USGS quadrant: Mount Mitchell
Access: Near Milepost 355 on the Blue Ridge Parkway, located 30 miles northeast of Asheville and 11.2 miles south of N.C. 80, turn north on to S.R. 218 and follow the signs for Mount Mitchell State Park. The northern trailhead is located on the Old Mount Mitchell Trail almost 0.2 mile south of the Mount Mitchell Summit Trail (N 35° 45' 49", W 82° 16' 2"). The southern trailhead is at the old Camp Alice, located off the Commissary Trail (N 35° 45' 27", W 82° 16' 6"). See map on page 199.

From the parking lot, follow the Mount Mitchell Summit Trail for 100 yards, then fork down to the right. After 0.2 mile, the Camp Alice Trail forks off to the left, following the blue, square blaze. The open, grassy trail descends through flowering raspberry and lady fern; much of it is shaded by a gorgeous canopy of Fraser fir, red spruce, and mountain ash. As you descend, you will enjoy spectacular views to the south of the Blue Ridge Mountains, including Green Knob at 145° and 3.7 miles. The trail switches back several times before ending at a T intersection with a gravel road; there is a nice stream to the left.

This is the former site of Camp Alice, a logging community in the 1920s. The dirt road to the left becomes the Buncombe Horse Trail as it wraps around Commissary Hill. After 0.3 mile on this dirt road, the Mountains-to-Sea Trail switches back to the right; after 0.9 mile, the Black Mountain Trail descends from the left. The dirt road to the right becomes the Commissary Trail, which ascends south for 1.2 miles to the Old Mount Mitchell Trail at the new ranger station in Stepps Gap.

COMMISSARY TRAIL

Length: 1.2 miles one way
Difficulty: easy
Elevation change: 250 feet
USGS quadrant: Mount Mitchell
Access: Near Milepost 355 on the Blue Ridge Parkway, located 30 miles northeast of Asheville and 11.2 miles south of N.C. 80, turn north on to S.R. 218 and follow the signs for Mount Mitchell State Park. The northern trailhead is located in Camp Alice (N 35° 45' 27", W 82° 16' 6"). The southern trailhead is located behind a gate to the right of the new ranger station in Stepps Gap; the station is approximately 2.6 miles from the junction with the Blue Ridge Parkway (N 35° 44' 44", W 82° 16' 38"). See map on page 199.

The Commissary Trail, a dirt road that connects Camp Alice to Stepps Gap, is useful in creating a loop trail. From the northern trailhead in Camp Alice, you will make a mellow ascent and enjoy spectacular views to the east and southeast of the Blue Ridge into McDowell County. The road is lined with red spruce, Fraser fir, white snakeroot, St.-John's-wort, oxalis, viburnum, and wood aster. After 1.2 miles, the trail ends behind a gate beside the ranger station. The mountain directly in front is

Clingmans Peak—not to be confused with Clingmans Dome, which is more than 70 miles to the west. The Old Mount Mitchell Trail, which begins on the other side of the ranger station, is marked by a wooden sign and a yellow dot beside the paved road.

OLD MOUNT MITCHELL TRAIL

Length: 2 miles one way
Difficulty: moderate
Elevation change: 400 feet
USGS quadrant: Mount Mitchell
Access: Near Milepost 355 on the Blue Ridge Parkway, located 30 miles northeast of Asheville and 11.2 miles south of N.C. 80, turn north on to S.R. 218 and follow the signs for Mount Mitchell State Park. The northern trailhead is on the Mount Mitchell Summit Trail 100 yards from the parking lot. The southern trailhead is to the left of the new ranger station in Stepps Gap; the station is approximately 2.6 miles from the junction with the Blue Ridge Parkway (N 35° 44' 44", W 82° 16' 38"). See map on page 199.

From the southern trailhead behind the ranger station, located 50 yards up the road from the parking lot, the yellow-blazed trail passes through a young spruce/fir forest and quickly begins a moderate-to-strenuous ascent. Along the way, you'll enjoy incredible views to the west and northwest across the Black Mountains and the Great Craggy Mountains. At 0.6 mile, the trail descends to the Mount Mitchell Restaurant, crosses the parking lot, and then resumes to the right. At 1 mile, it heads alongside the paved road for 100 yards, then veers to the right toward the tent camping area—the only place in the state park where camping is allowed. The Camp Alice Trail ascends

from the right at 1.8 miles. Two tenths of a mile later, the Old
Mount Mitchell Trail ends at a **T** intersection with the Mount
Mitchell Summit Trail.

MOUNT MITCHELL LOOP
Length: 4.6 miles
Difficulty: moderate
Elevation change: 900 feet
USGS quadrant: Mount Mitchell
Access: Near Milepost 355 on the Blue Ridge Parkway,
    located 30 miles northeast of Asheville and 11.2
    miles south of N.C. 80, turn north on to S.R. 218 and
    follow the signs for Mount Mitchell State Park. See
    map on page 199.

It is possible to combine
the previous three trails into
an excellent 4.6-mile loop.
From the summit parking lot,
follow the Mount Mitchell
Summit Trail for 100 yards,
then turn right on to the Camp
Alice Trail. Follow the Camp
Alice Trail to its end, then turn
right on to the Commissary
Trail. At the ranger station,
turn right on the Old Mount
Mitchell Trail, which will
bring you back to the starting
point.

*James Hamrick on Old Mount
Mitchell Trail*

Tick-Borne Illnesses
in the North Carolina Mountains

Ticks are responsible for transmitting a number of infectious diseases, including Rocky Mountain spotted fever, Lyme disease, babesiosis, erhlichiosis, tularemia, Colorado tick fever, and others. Fortunately, only about 5 percent of ticks shepherd the microorganisms that are responsible for disease. The two most common tick-borne diseases in the North Carolina mountains are Rocky Mountain spotted fever and erhlichiosis.

Rocky Mountain spotted fever (RMSF) is a bit of a misnomer. Most infections are actually acquired in the Southeast, not in the Rocky Mountains. RMSF has a seasonal character, most cases occurring between April and September. One of the ticks that transmits this disease is *Dermacentor variabilis*, also known as the common dog tick. This tick is large and grayish black. RMSF is also carried by *Amblyomma americanum*, the Lone Star tick, a smaller, brownish orange tick with a white spot on its back. A tick must be attached to its human host for at least six hours and ideally for 24 hours before it can transmit the infectious agent. The first symptoms of RMSF appear four to 10 days after the exposure. They include fever (often greater than 102 degrees), headache, muscle aches, and a rash. The rash may be delayed a few days but occurs in approximately 90 percent of patients. It consists of small, flat, red or purple patches and begins on the wrists and ankles and spreads inward. Prompt treatment of RMSF with appropriate antibiotics is important; the mortality rate has been reduced from 25 percent to 5 percent with therapy. Survivors develop immunity against further attacks.

Erhlichiosis was not described until 1987. It is found mainly in the Southeast. It is transmitted by the same ticks that transmit RMSF and has the same seasonal distribution. The symptoms resemble those of RMSF, except that a rash develops in only 20 percent of those infected. This has prompted some physicians to call this disease "Rocky Mountain spotless fever"! Headache, high fever, and muscle aches usually occur seven to 11 days after the tick bite. The symptoms last one to two weeks and are often milder than those of RMSF, although there is an aggressive and often fatal form of erhlichiosis. As with RMSF, prompt recognition and antibiotic treatment are important.

Lyme disease is highly publicized but actually occurs very rarely in North Carolina. It is much more common in the Northeast. It is transmitted by *Ixodes scapularis*, the deer tick, which is tiny and brown-black in color. A rash appears within seven to 10 days of the tick bite. Known as erythema migrans, this rash is characterized by a ringed lesion around the bite. Other symptoms include enlarged lymph nodes close to the bite, low-grade fever, fatigue, and joint and muscle pain. The late stages of the disease can involve the central nervous system and the joints and can even cause cardiac arrhythmias. Lyme disease may also be treated with specific antibiotics.

Tularemia, also known as "rabbit fever," is of minor importance to hikers. This tick-borne illness is transmitted by the same ticks as RMSF and erhlichiosis. It can also be contracted by handling the tissues of infected animals; the classical case is of hunters who skin wild rabbits. Typically, an ulcer develops within 24 to 48 hours at the site of the tick bite. Fever and swollen lymph nodes are present. Tularemia has a low fatality rate (1 percent) and responds to specific antibiotics.

At the time of this writing, there was emerging evidence of a new Lyme disease–like tick-borne illness in the South. The Lone Star tick is most likely responsible for transmitting this new disease, known currently as "Southern tick illness." The clinical

continued

symptoms and treatment are similar to those of Lyme disease.

Protection against ticks is imperative. Hikers should wear light-colored clothing that make ticks noticeable. They should also tuck their long pants into their socks. They should use tick repellents that contain DEET on their skin and repellents that contain Permethrin on their clothes. They should conduct tick checks, paying close attention to the scalp, every few hours. If an embedded tick is discovered, it should be removed promptly with tweezers. Grasp the tick close to the skin and pull upward with steady pressure; be careful not to leave any parts embedded. Hikers should note the date of exposure in the event that symptoms develop that could be caused by a tick-borne illness.

ROAN MOUNTAIN STATE PARK

Roan Mountain has long been famous for its sweeping canopies of *Rhododendron catawbiense*. In fact, John Muir wrote about the brilliant mountain during one of his trips back east. There are two short hikes within Roan Mountain State Park. The fee for entering the state park was three dollars per car at the time of this book's publication.

Rhododendron abounds on Roan Mountain
PHOTO BY CAROLYN SAKOWSKI

CLOUDLAND TRAIL (#171)

Length: 1.2 miles one way
Difficulty: easy
Elevation change: 140 feet
USGS quadrant: Bakersville
Access: From Bakersville, take N.C. 261 north to Carver's
Gap, located just before the Tennessee border. Turn
left on the park road, following the signs for Roan
High Gardens. The trail begins beside a wooden sign
at the northern end of the paved parking lot (N 36°
06' 15", W 82° 07' 59"). The trail at the other end of
the parking lot is the Appalachian Trail.

The trail follows an easy north-northeast ascent to a spectacular overlook, passing through lots of Fraser fir, rhododendron, Canadian mayflower, spring beauty, Southern lady and
cinnamon fern, St.-John's-wort, May apple, mountain ash,
speckled wood lily, club moss, bluets, gooseberry, yarrow,
moosewood, blueberry, and false hellebore along the way. The
trail forks after 100 yards. To the right, a short spur trail leads
to an overlook facing north; the main trail continues straight
ahead. The Rhododendron Gardens Trail comes in from the
left at 0.3 mile. You will cross a road at 0.5 mile and again 0.2
mile later. The trail ends at 1.2 miles at a large wooden observation deck that offers a stunning panorama to the north (N 05'
35", W 08' 45"). You'll see Mount Mitchell at 201° and 23.6
miles, Mount Pisgah at 221° and 57.4 miles, High Peak in the

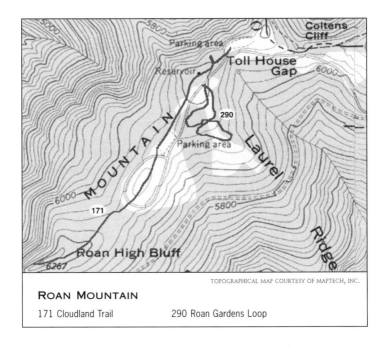

TOPOGRAPHICAL MAP COURTESY OF MAPTECH, INC.

ROAN MOUNTAIN

171 Cloudland Trail   290 Roan Gardens Loop

Cane Mountains at 241° and 14.6 miles, Mount Sterling at 248° and 60.9 miles, Max Patch at 250° and 49.7 miles, Mount Guyot at 251° and 67.7 miles, Big Bald in the Bald Mountains at 254° and 20.5 miles, the Unaka Mountains and the Nolichucky River Gorge at 276° and 13.5 miles, Shepherd Knob at 285° and 4.2 miles, Little Bald Knob in the Iron Mountains at 300° and 6.1 miles, Little Rock Knob at 3° and 3.9 miles, and White Rock at 13° and 10.2 miles.

ROAN GARDENS LOOP (#290)

Length: 0.3 or 0.9 mile round trip
Difficulty: easy
Elevation change: 80 feet
USGS quadrant: Bakersville
Access: From Bakersville, take N.C. 261 north to Carver's
Gap, located just before the Tennessee border. Turn
left, following the signs to Roan High Gardens. Turn
left on to the dirt road just before the paved parking
lot. The trail begins on the left beside the visitor
center (N 36° 06' 7", W 82° 08' 6").

There are actually two loops here—an 0.3-mile handi-
capped-accessible interpretive trail and a longer figure-eight
option that is also paved but in slight disrepair. The first point
of interest is Overlook #16, which offers a sweeping view to
the south overlooking a hillside of Catawba rhododendron,
blackberry, and mountain ash. From here, you can see Little
Yellow Mountain at 128° and 4.4 miles, Hawk Mountain at 139°
and 4.5 miles, Rock Creek Mountain at 172° and 3.5 miles, and
a mine scar on Wilson Knob at 182° and 7.8 miles. The trail
forks 20 yards past Overlook #16. The interpretive hike breaks
off to the right; the longer loop continues straight ahead and
eventually returns to this point after 0.5 mile.

Camping, Biking, Fishing, and Hunting

Pisgah National Forest offers many opportunities for recreation.

Camping is available in a variety of settings that range from isolated back-country sites to sites complete with restrooms, picnic tables, and RV hookups. In addition, camping is allowed in many areas of the national forest that are not developed campgrounds; no permit is required. Permits are required for camping in the Linville Gorge Wilderness on weekends and holidays from May 1 to October 31; they may be obtained in advance from the ranger station in the Grandfather Ranger District.

Mountain biking is allowed on over 235 miles of trails in Pisgah National Forest outside of designated wilderness areas. Trails open to bicyclists are designated by the bike symbol. There are many miles of "bike-able" trails in the Pisgah Ranger District.

Fishing and hunting are permitted in parts of Pisgah National Forest under the regulation of the North Carolina Wildlife Resources Commission. Both activities require licenses and are strictly regulated to ensure preservation of wildlife and safety for all users of the national forest. The most comprehensive source for hunting and fishing information is the *Regulations Digest*. For a copy, write or call North Carolina Wildlife Resources Commission, 512 North Salisbury Street, Raleigh, N.C. 27604-1188 (919-662-4381).

Detailed information on camping, biking, fishing, hunting, and other activities in Pisgah National Forest can be obtained from the following sources.

On the web:
www.cs.unca.edu/nfsnc (official web site of the national forests in North Carolina)

continued

French Broad Ranger District
P.O. Box 128
Hot Springs, N.C. 28743
(828) 622-3202
  The office is located on
U.S. 25/70 in Hot Springs.

Toecane Ranger District
P.O. Box 128
Burnsville, N.C. 28714
(828) 682-6146
  The office is located on
U.S. 19-E Bypass in Burnsville.

Grandfather Ranger District
Route 1, Box 110-A
Nebo, N.C. 28761
(828) 652-2144
  The office is located at Exit
90 (the Nebo/Lake James exit)
off Interstate 40 some 9 miles
east of Marion.

Pisgah Ranger District
1001 Pisgah Highway
Pisgah Forest, N.C. 28768
(828) 877-3350
  The office is located on
U.S. 276 north of Brevard.

OTHER TRAILS IN THE
TOECANE RANGER DISTRICT

BALD KNOB RIDGE TRAIL (#186)
Length: 2.8 miles one way
Difficulty: moderate
Elevation change: 1,400 feet
USGS quadrants: Montreat, Old Fort
Access: The trail begins at the small pull-off on the
        northeastern side of the Blue Ridge Parkway near
        Milepost 355, located 0.4 mile south of Mount
        Mitchell State Park (N 35° 42' 54", W 82° 16' 26").

This excellent trail descends through a large grove of virgin spruce/fir to the headwaters of the South Toe River. It begins by heading perpendicularly away from the parkway down the spine of the ridge. After 0.1 mile, you will enter the national forest and pass the remains of an old cabin to your left. The trail begins an easy-to-moderate descent through a lush canopy of pine, hemlock, and mountain ash. After 0.4 mile, the terrain levels out; you will pass by some good places to camp. A quarter-mile later, the trail veers to the right as it passes south of a ridge knob. Shortly thereafter, you will enter a virgin grove of red spruce and Fraser fir. This primeval forest is perpetually

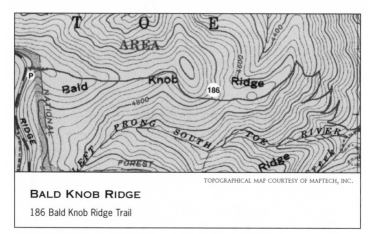

BALD KNOB RIDGE

186 Bald Knob Ridge Trail

TOPOGRAPHICAL MAP COURTESY OF MAPTECH, INC.

dark and moist; it drips with mysterious mosses and ferns, violets, trillium, umbrella-leaf, galax, yellow bead lily, bluets, partridgeberry, wood sorrel, and Canadian mayflower. Three tenths of a mile later, the trail leaves the grove and passes beneath a laurel slick. Around 1.5 miles, it switches down to the right and begins a series of long switchbacks among rhododendron, moosewood, Dutchman's-pipe, mountain maple, serviceberry, wild hydrangea, and flame azalea. Half a mile later, it briefly follows an old roadbed. It merges on to a larger old road at 2.6 miles and follows it for nearly 0.2 mile to the trail's end on F.R. 472, marked by a carsonite sign. Across the road, the Left Prong of the South Toe merges with Hemphill Creek to create the South Toe River.

Length: 0.2 mile one way
Difficulty: easy
Elevation change: 80 feet
USGS quadrangle: Elk Park
Access: From Spruce Pine, head north on U.S. 19E
for approximately 20 miles to the town of
Cranberry. Continue approximately 1.3 miles on
U.S. 19E to the junction with N.C. 194 North (not
N.C. 194 South). From the junction, continue
straight ahead on U.S. 19E for 0.7 mile, then turn
right on to Old Mill Road just past the Avery
County Rescue Squad building. You will soon
begin to see signs for Elk River Falls. After 0.4
mile, turn right on Elk River Road (S.R. 1305).
Drive 4.2 miles to the parking lot at the end of
the road (N 36° 11' 50", W 81° 58' 12").

The trail ascends a short series of steps and reaches the top of the falls at 0.1 mile. To the left, it descends to a large rock spit that juts into water near the base of the falls. This is unquestionably one of the most beautiful falls in North Carolina. The Elk River drops 65 feet into a solid-rock amphitheater. The rock spit encloses the water, creating a truly perfect swimming hole. Given the splendor of the falls and the shortness of the trail,

Elk Falls
PHOTO BY CAROLYN SAKOWSKI

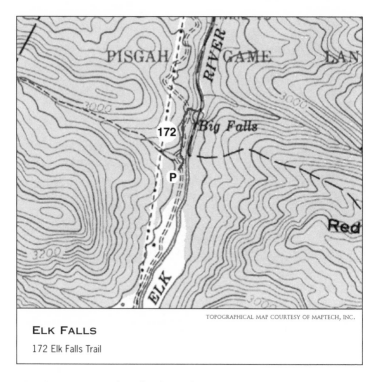

ELK FALLS

172 Elk Falls Trail

it isn't surprising that this hike draws crowds; while the beauty here is considerable, solitude is hard to find.

FRENCH BROAD

RANGER

DISTRICT

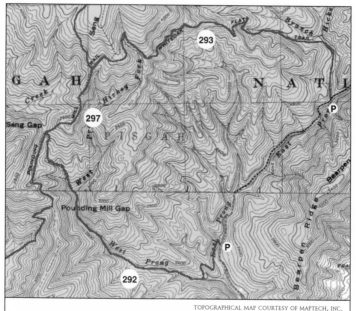

TOPOGRAPHICAL MAP COURTESY OF MAPTECH, INC.

HICKEY FORK LOOP

292 Hickey Fork Trail   293 White Oak Trail

297 Pounding Mill Trail

Hickey Fork Area

Hickey Fork Trail (#292)

Length: 2.3 miles one way
Difficulty: moderate, with a few strenuous sections
Elevation change: 1,200 feet
USGS quadrangles: White Rock, Greystone
Access: Turn northwest off U.S. 25/U.S. 70 on to N.C.
280. Drive 3.5 miles, then turn right on N.C. 212. Go
7 miles, then turn left on Hickey Fork Road (S.R.
1310) at the brown Forest Service sign 0.2 mile past
Cutshall's Grocery. Proceed 1.2 miles down the dirt
road to the parking area on the right. The trailhead is
60 feet farther on the left at a carsonite sign (N 35°
59' 41", W 82° 42' 17").

The yellow-blazed Hickey Fork Trail begins after you cross a slippery wooden bridge over Hickey Fork. The narrow, easy trail enters a deep, perpetually moist valley of tall hemlock; it is lined with a variety of wildflowers such as foamflower, violets, wild geranium, doll's eye, houstonia, jack-in-the-pulpit, goatsbeard, dog-hobble, rhododendron, and Southern lady fern. After a switchback, the trail crosses a stream at 0.4 mile (N 59'

36", W 42' 25"); it crosses again 0.1 mile later (N 59' 32", W 42' 24"). The trail, lined with partridgeberry, wood and rue anemone, trillium, and wild hydrangea, then crosses several small springs. The ascent becomes moderate at 1.3 miles. Here, you'll see a scenic water slide over 100 feet long (N 59' 39", W 42' 58"). A hundred yards upstream is a beautiful cascade down a large rock outcropping; look for Indian cucumber, mountain laurel, false Solomon's-seal, star chickweed, and blue cohosh. The trail reaches a patch of stinging nettles at 1.6 miles. You will cross a small branch from the left 100 yards later, then cross another spring from the right 100 yards after that. From here, you will make a strenuous ascent along the right side of the prong. The trail switches back at 2 miles, leaves the water, and enters a mixed hardwood forest with lots of alternate-leaved dogwood, mountain spiderwort, and monarda (N 0' 9", W 43' 28"). A quarter-mile later, the trail ends at T intersection with the Pounding Mill Trail in Seng Gap (N 0' 19", W 43' 29"); a small campsite is located here. To continue the loop trail, turn right on the Pounding Mill Trail.

WHITE OAK TRAIL (#293)

Length: 2.2 miles one way
Difficulty: moderate
Elevation change: 1,100 feet
USGS quadrangle: Greystone
Access: Turn northwest off U.S. 25/U.S. 70 on to N.C.
   280. Drive 3.5 miles, then turn right on N.C. 212. Go
   7 miles, then turn left on Hickey Fork Road (S.R.
   1310) at the brown Forest Service sign 0.2 mile past
   Cutshall's Grocery. Proceed 2.5 miles down the dirt
   road, then turn left when the road forks. Six-tenths of
   a mile later, you will come to a cul-de-sac. The White
   Oak Trail, marked by a carsonite sign, begins directly
   in front (N 35° 0' 49", W 82° 41' 43").

From the trailhead on the Pounding Mill Trail, the blue-blazed White Oak Trail begins an easy descent on an old roadbed through sassafras, beech, and lots of flame azalea. It makes a sharp bend to the right after 0.25 mile, leaves the roadbed, and descends into the cove of the West Prong of Hickey Fork (N 0' 45", W 42' 0"). Two tenths of a mile later, you will cross a small spring marked by pink tape on a yellow birch (N 0' 51", W 42' 57"). The trail switches back to the left and leaves the cove at 0.5 mile (N 0' 43", W 42' 47"). Thereafter, you will have nice views to the southeast of Bearpen Ridge. Half a mile later, the descent becomes moderate. You will reach a gravel road at 1.4 miles (N 0' 51", W 42' 10"). Here, the trail makes a sharp bend to the left and descends away from the road into Big Rocky Branch Cove. After negotiating a series of switchbacks and treacherous amounts of stinging nettles, you will reach the valley bottom and veer to the right at 1.8 miles. A carsonite sign at

2.2 miles marks the trail's eastern terminus at a gravel-road intersection (N 0' 49", W 41' 43"). To the left is a cul-de-sac; to the right is a gated road. Continue straight ahead down the gravel road, past lots of goat's-rue. The gravel road merges with Hickey Fork Road after 0.6 mile. There is a great swimming and fishing hole 0.3 mile later. You will return to the parking area for the Hickey Fork Trail at 1.9 miles. (This location is 4.1 miles from the trailhead for Pounding Mill Trail.)

POUNDING MILL TRAIL (#297)

Length: 6.4 miles one way
Difficulty: moderate to strenuous
Elevation change: 2,900 feet
USGS quadrangles: Greystone, White Rock, Hot Springs
Access: Turn northwest off U.S. 25/U.S. 70 on to N.C.
    208 and drive 7.2 miles to the small, unmarked
    turnout on the left 2.2 miles east of the Tennessee
    border. The trail begins at the base of a steep, old
    logging road on the right; there is no trail sign (N 35°
    58' 37", 82° 45' 17").

This is a very faint, seldom-used trail through remote, wild Madison County. It offers outstanding views, flora, and abundant wildlife—notably pheasant and grouse, among others. The trail is best hiked in the months when the foliage does not obstruct the views and the stinging nettles aren't thick.

Begin by climbing the logging road for 100 yards to a three-way fork; the trail begins on the middle fork. It is marked by orange blazes, but you'll need luck to find any of them. The trail follows the dirt road for the first 0.3 mile, then passes beneath a dense canopy of rhododendron; poison ivy, stinging

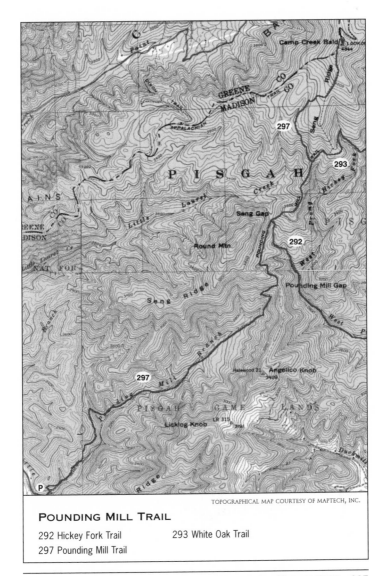

POUNDING MILL TRAIL

292 Hickey Fork Trail   293 White Oak Trail

297 Pounding Mill Trail

nettles, white pine, hemlock, cucumber tree, cinquefoil, creeping cedar, hedge nettles, whorled loosestrife, wild geranium, spiderwort, partridgeberry, trillium, crested dwarf iris, and white monarda are but a few of the plants that line the old roadbed. The trail bends sharply to the right after 0.8 mile; an old footpath continues straight ahead. Fifteen yards later, you will cross a small branch. You will then come to a creek crossing at 1.4 miles where you'll see the remnants of an old footbridge; using the bridge is ill advised (N 59' 15", W 44' 28"). Once you reach the other side, you will ascend to the right of the branch through lots of dog-hobble, goatsbeard, and Solomon's-seal; though the easy-to-moderate ascent follows an old roadbed, it has become so overgrown that it can be difficult to follow. The trail enters a tulip poplar grove and crosses Pounding Mill Branch at 1.9 miles. You will cross the branch again 0.1 mile later. Thereafter, the moderate ascent is plagued by patches of poison ivy. At 3.1 miles, the trail switches back to the left and makes a moderate-to-strenuous ascent through lots of wood betony, houstonia, and fire pink. It continues to switch back for the next 0.25 mile before reaching an old roadbed at 3.4 miles (N 59' 53", W 43' 25"). The Pounding Mill Trail follows the road to the left. (To the right, the road leads to Angelico Knob. After 0.5 mile, it bends left at a rusty metal pole. If you're feeling adventurous, you can bushwhack to the right through stinging nettles to reach the summit. The road continues 1.4 miles down to Duckmill Creek Road.)

The Pounding Mill Trail reaches an old, small campsite in Seng Gap at 4 miles (N 0' 19", W 43' 29"). The Hickory Fork

Trail, marked by a yellow blaze on a hickory tree, descends to the right. The Pounding Mill Trail continues a moderate ascent of Seng Ridge through flame azalea, maple-leaved viburnum, wild hydrangea, mountain laurel, and bowman's root. It offers excellent views of the Bald Mountains of Tennessee to the left. The White Oak Trail, marked by a carsonite sign, forks off to the right at 4.7 miles (N 0' 40", W 43' 10"). About 0.6 mile later, the trail narrows to a single track. It intersects the Appalachian Trail at 6.3 miles (N 1' 17", W 42' 58") and continues straight ahead. A tenth of a mile later, it reaches the tower area. There are several towers here, only one of which is accessible to the public. To reach the lookout tower, loop around to the right for 100 yards. From the stairwell, you will see Blaxter Cliff at 72° and 1.4 miles; Roan High Knob at 85° and 33.6 miles; Big Knob of Bearpen Ridge (overlooking the valley of the East Prong of Little Prong) at 107° and 2.3 miles; Sugarloaf at 115° and 6 miles; Celo Knob at 119° and 28.6 miles; Mount Mitchell at 130° and 30.9 miles; Devil's Den at 163° and 10 miles and Highrock at 177° and 10 miles, both in the Walnut Mountains; Mount Pisgah at 188° and 41.3 miles; Balsam Knob at 203° and 47.9 miles; Max Patch at 225° and 20.7 miles; Mount Sterling at 230° and 31.8 miles; Mount Le Conte at 242° and 47.8 miles; Mount Guyot at 238° and 37.5 miles; and Greene Mountain at 281° and 2.6 miles.

HICKEY FORK LOOP

Length: 7.1 miles or 10.5 miles round trip
Difficulty: moderate
Elevation change: 1,650 feet
USGS quadrangles: White Rock, Greystone
Access: Turn northwest off U.S. 25/U.S. 70 on to N.C.
  280. Drive 3.5 miles, then turn right on N.C. 212. Go
  7 miles, then turn left on Hickey Fork Road (S.R.
  1310) at the brown Forest Service sign 0.2 mile past
  Cutshall's Grocery. Proceed 1.2 miles down the dirt
  road to the parking area on the right. The trailhead is
  60 feet farther on the left at a carsonite sign (N 35°
  59' 41", W 82° 42' 17"). See map on page 220.

This is an excellent day hike up one creek valley, along a ridge top, and down a second creek valley. It offers excellent wildflower diversity, views of wild Madison County and Tennessee, and lots of wildlife. *Caution*: Do not wear shorts on this hike! Both the Hickey Fork Trail and the White Oak Trail have 0.25-mile patches of thigh-high stinging nettles. You should wear long pants.

The loop begins with the Hickey Fork Trail and follows it until it ends on the Pounding Mill Trail. Turn right on the Pounding Mill Trail and continue 0.7 mile before turning right on the White Oak Trail. Follow the White Oak Trail back to the Forest Service road. Turn right to return to the parking area for the Hickey Fork Trail.

If you have the time and energy to hike 10.5 miles round trip, it is highly recommended that you follow the Pounding Mill Trail all the way to Camp Creek Bald and then backtrack before you turn on to the White Oak Trail.

MAX PATCH AREA

CHERRY CREEK TRAIL (#300)

Length: 1.8 miles one way
Difficulty: moderate to strenuous
Elevation change: 1,350 feet
USGS quadrant: Lemon Gap
Access: Take Exit #7 off Interstate 40 and turn right on to
Cold Springs Creek Road. A hundred yards later, the
pavement ends and F.R. 148 begins. From the end of
the pavement, it is 4.5 miles to the trailhead for
Cherry Creek Trail (N 35° 46' 10", W 82° 58' 18").
The easily missed trailhead is on the left; park in the
large gravel pull-out on the right. Two tenths of a mile
farther up the road is the gated F.R. 3532.

The Cherry Creek Trail is marked by blue blazes, but good
luck finding any of them. You will begin a moderate ascent on
a narrow trail that runs parallel to narrow, high-volume Cherry
Creek. The path is lined with jewelweed, phacelia, poison ivy,
sedum, wild geranium, meadow rue, orchids, and foamflower.
It is used by equestrians, so some sections will likely be rather
muddy. At 0.2 mile, you will cross a large branch and come to

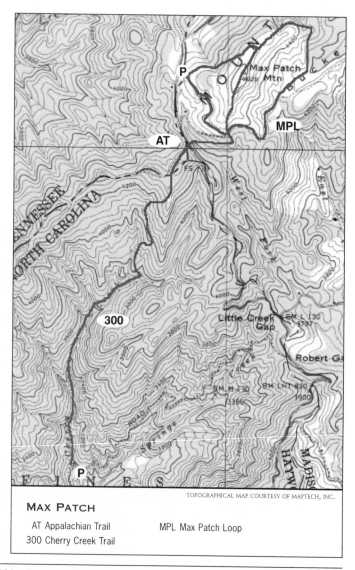

MAX PATCH

TOPOGRAPHICAL MAP COURTESY OF MAPTECH, INC.

AT Appalachian Trail
300 Cherry Creek Trail

MPL Max Patch Loop

F.R. 3532; go about 10 yards to the right, then turn left on to the trail again. From here, the trail begins an easy-to-moderate ascent through hawthorn, dogwood, Carolina silverbell, rhododendron, flame azalea, Clinton's lily, various trilliums, true and false Solomon's-seal, doll's eye, star chickweed, and bee balm; to your right, the gorgeous Cherry Creek cascades over moss-entombed rocks. For the next 0.5 mile, you will follow a moderate ascent through Cherry Cove and cross a few small branches descending from the left. At 1 mile, you will cross a creek. Ahead, the trail switches back sharply to the left and ascends through galax, mountain laurel, elm, umbrella magnolia, and flame azalea. About 0.3 mile later, it enters a magnificent stand of old-growth hemlock, then switches back to the right. At 1.5 miles, you will come to F.R. 3533, a grassy, overgrown, gravel road marked by a carsonite sign. The trail follows the road for 25 yards to the left, past lots of false downy foxglove, then forks to the right. About 0.1 mile later, you will turn right on to an old roadbed. At 1.8 miles, a second roadbed forks down to the right, while the trail continues to the left. Fifty yards later, it ends at a campsite and a T intersection with the Appalachian Trail (N 47' 24", W 57' 48"); the intersection is marked by a wooden sign reading "Cherry Creek." To reach Max Patch, turn right on to the Appalachian Trail.

MAX PATCH SUMMIT VIA APPALACHIAN TRAIL

Length: 2 miles one way
Difficulty: moderate
Elevation change: 430 feet
USGS quadrant: Lemon Gap
Access: This hike begins where the previous one ended—
at the junction of the Cherry Creek Trail and the
Appalachian Trail.

Follow the white-blazed Appalachian Trail to the major junction after 0.2 mile. Here, two roads descend to the left and Max Patch Road ascends straight ahead to the left before descending back to the right. The Appalachian Trail resumes to your right on the other side of Max Patch Road, behind a horse gate and a white blaze. You will cross a delightful, bubbling branch surrounded by Turk's-cap lily, then begin an easy-to-moderate ascent alongside a barbed-wire fence. You will cross a gravel road and come to a trail junction marked by a rather complicated wooden sign at 0.6 mile (N 47' 34", W 57' 29"). To the left, it is 0.4 mile to the Max Patch Parking Lot; it is 2 miles to the same parking lot via the trail to the right; the Appalachian Trail continues straight ahead 0.4 mile to the Max Patch summit. The summit is an open, breezy, grass bald blanketed with yarrow, horse nettles, buttercups, different violets, and other small flowers. In the 1800s, the mountain was cleared for grazing. In a more recent, more daring time, it was used as a landing field for small aircraft. From the summit, you will enjoy truly awe-inspiring views in all directions. Beginning to the north, you will see Round Mountain at 3° and 3.6 miles, Chucky Mountain at 18° and 14 miles, Camp Creek Bald at 45° and

20.7 miles, Bluff Mountain at 47° and 4.1 miles, Rich Mountain at 49° and 25.9 miles, Sugarloaf Knob at 59° and 23.4 miles, Lick Rock at 61° and 23.2 miles, Big Bald at 67° and 29.3 miles, Upper Haw Knob at 71° and 28 miles, Celo Knob at 89° and 39.8 miles, Coxcomb Mountain at 92° and 32.7 miles, Mount Mitchell at 98° and 38.9 miles, Craggy Knob at 107° and 32.9 miles, Mikes Knob at 126° and 8.8 miles, Sandymush Bald at 157° and 9.1 miles, Mount Pisgah at 161° and 28 miles, Crabtree Bald at 171° and 10.5 miles, Cold Mountain at 172° and 27.3 miles, Shining Rock at 174° and 30.1 miles, Black Balsam Knob at 176° and 32.7 miles, High Top at 180° and 28.6 miles, Mount Hardy at 181° and 34.1 miles, Lickstone Bald at 186° and 25.7 miles, Richland Balsam at 188° and 29.7 miles, Grassy Bald at 196° and 26.5 miles, Waterrock Knob at 208° and 25.1 miles, Mount Sterling at 239° and 11.4 miles, Luftee Knob at 248° and 16.2 miles, Mount Guyot at 253° and 18 miles, Cammer Ridge at 260° and 12 miles, and Hall Mountain at 298° and 11.5 miles. From the summit, the Appalachian Trail descends 0.1 mile to a second junction with the Max Patch Loop Trail; the junction is marked by a wooden sign. The Appalachian Trail and the Max Patch Trail run conjunctively for the next 0.9 mile, where-upon the Appalachian Trail forks off to the left and the Max Patch Loop Trail turns to the right and overlaps the Buckeye Ridge Trail.

Length: 2.4 miles round trip; 2.6 miles if you go to the
    summit
Difficulty: easy to moderate
Elevation change: 320 feet
USGS quadrant: Lemon Gap
Access: Take Exit #7 off Interstate 40 and turn right on to
    Cold Springs Creek Road. A hundred yards later, the
    pavement ends and F.R. 148 begins. Follow F.R. 148
    for 6.2 miles, then turn left on Max Patch Road (S.R.
    1182). The Max Patch Parking Lot is 2 miles ahead.

If you take the left fork from the parking area, you will
begin an easy-to-moderate ascent along the western slope of
Max Patch. You will reach a T intersection with the Appalachian Trail at 0.5 mile; the junction is marked by a wooden
sign. The summit is 0.1 mile to the right; the Max Patch Loop
Trail runs conjunctively with the Appalachian Trail to the left.
You will descend to a campsite in a maple grove at 0.8 mile.
The trail then veers to the right and descends into a small cove.
After 0.1 mile, you will cross a small spring lined with bee balm,
goat's-rue, umbrella-leaf, jewelweed, and rhododendron. The
trail passes a nice campsite beneath a large maple 0.2 mile later;
the remains of an old fence stand to the left. From here, you
will ascend through wood fern, club moss, rhododendron, and
other heath genera before turning right on to an old roadbed
marked by a wooden sign at 1.2 miles; this is the halfway point
of the loop. You will then continue a southerly trek for almost
0.25 mile through flame azalea, viburnum, white snakeroot,
blueberry, and moosewood; keep your eye out for deer and
grouse. You will then come to a T intersection with the Buckeye

View of Pisgah National Forest

Ridge Trail, a dirt road popular among equestrians. The Appalachian Trail turns to the left; the Max Patch Trail and the Buckeye Ridge Trail run conjunctively to the right. You will make an easy-to-moderate ascent on the old gravel road. The Buckeye Ridge Trail forks to the left beneath a large red maple at 1.7 miles; the fork is marked by a carsonite sign. (The Buckeye Ridge Trail follows a moderate descent beneath a dense canopy of rhododendron, crosses a stream 0.4 mile later, and ends at Max Patch Road at 0.6 mile.) The Max Patch Loop Trail veers sharply to the right at the fork. Three tenths of a mile later, it comes to a large junction marked by a rather chatty wooden sign. The dirt road continues straight ahead to Max Patch Road (S.R. 1182); the Appalachian Trail ascends from the left and continues to the right toward the summit; and the Max Patch Trail veers off to the right. From the sign, you will gradually descend around the southwestern slope of Max Patch through lots of blueberry before returning to the parking lot 0.4 mile later.

As the billboard at the parking lot indicates, there are two loop options here. The 2.4-mile loop is described above. The 1.4-mile loop omits the back 1.5 miles of the Max Patch Loop Trail in favor of the 0.5 mile of the Appalachian Trail that crests the summit of Max Patch. If you take the right fork from the parking area, it is 0.4 mile to the junction with the Appalachian Trail. Turn left on the Appalachian Trail. You will crest the summit at 0.8 mile. You should then turn left back on to the Max Patch Loop Trail at 0.9 mile to return to the parking lot 0.5 mile later.

CHERRY CREEK TRAIL/APPALACHIAN TRAIL LOOP

Length: 6.8 miles round trip
Difficulty: moderate to strenuous
Elevation change: 1,630 feet
USGS quadrant: Lemon Gap

In addition to the 1.4-mile and 2.4-mile loop trails described above, you can combine the Cherry Creek Trail and the Appalachian Trail to create an incredible full-day hike. Follow the Cherry Creek Trail for 1.8 miles, then turn right on the Appalachian Trail. Take the Appalachian Trail over the Max Patch summit to the Buckeye Ridge Trail at 3.8 miles, then turn right on the Max Patch Loop Trail. Follow the Max Patch Loop Trail back to the intersection with the Appalachian Trail at 4.4 miles. Turn left on the Appalachian Trail. Backtrack 0.6 mile on the

Appalachian Trail, then turn left on to the Cherry Gap Trail at 5 miles and follow it back to the starting point.

Previously, it was possible to make a full-day, strenuous, 7.5-mile loop by combining the Cherry Creek Trail, the Appalachian Trail, the Max Patch Loop Trail, and the now-defunct Cherry Ridge Trail. If you are the type who can't resist some serious bushwhacking, you can still attempt it, though you may not get very far on the Cherry Ridge Trail.

Follow the Cherry Creek Trail for 1.8 miles, then turn right on the Appalachian Trail. Take the Appalachian Trail over the Max Patch summit to the Buckeye Ridge Trail at 3.8 miles. Turn right on the Max Patch Loop Trail/Buckeye Ridge Trail. The two trails run conjunctively for 0.3 mile. Follow the Buckeye Gap Trail when it forks off to the left. The Buckeye Ridge Trail ends 0.6 mile later on Max Patch Road. Turn left and walk down the road for 0.6 mile, then turn right at the large turnaround and horse tie. The Cherry Ridge Trail begins to the far right and descends 1.1 miles to F.R. 148. *If* you can reach F.R. 148, turn right; it is 1.1 miles back to the beginning of the Cherry Creek Trail.

Where Am I?

What is the difference between a *national forest* and a *national park*?

A national forest is designated by the United States Department of Agriculture as a "land of many uses." This specification is intended to promote *conservation* of the land. National forests were originally created to protect water quality and to provide a continuous supply of timber. They allow for resource extraction and recreation. They also provide a habitat for wildlife. Visitors may enjoy scenic drives, hiking trails, hunting, fishing, swimming, car camping, and mountain biking and other off-road activities in designated areas. North Carolina has four national forests totaling 1.2 million acres. They are Nantahala National Forest, Pisgah National Forest, Croatan National Forest, and Uwharrie National Forest. Pisgah, the oldest, is comprised of four districts: the Pisgah Ranger District, the Grandfather Ranger District, the Toecane Ranger District, and the French Broad Ranger District. Back-country permits are not required in Pisgah National Forest except in the Linville Gorge Wilderness Area.

A national park is designated by the United States Department of Interior for *preservation* of the land. There are strict controls over the use of the land in our national parks. No hunting, no off-road vehicles or mountain bikes, no car camping except in designated campgrounds, and no resource extraction are allowed. Backcountry camping is allowed with a permit.

What is a *wilderness area*?

A wilderness area is an area within a national forest that is given the same protection and operates under similar regulations as a national park. Hunting and fishing may be restricted. The objective is to preserve an area of natural or historical significance. There are three wilderness areas in Pisgah National Forest: Middle Prong Wilderness Area, Shining Rock Wilderness Area, and Linville Gorge Wilderness Area. There are legislative plans for additional wilderness areas, at Lost Cove and Harper Creek.

OTHER TRAILS IN THE FRENCH BROAD RANGER DISTRICT

LOVER'S LEAP TRAIL (#308)

Length: 1.6 miles round trip
Difficulty: strenuous for the first 0.5 mile, easy thereafter
Elevation change: 450 feet
USGS quadrangle: Hot Springs
Access: From the town of Hot Springs, head southeast on U.S. 25/U.S. 70. Immediately after crossing the French Broad River, turn right (north) on Paint Creek Road. There is no road sign here; look for a historical marker for Paint Rock and a sign for Hot Springs Freewill Baptist Church. Drive almost 0.1 mile, then take the first left. Follow this road for 0.25 mile to just past where the pavement ends. A parking area is on the left. The trailhead is on the right (N 35° 53' 32", W 82° 49' 3").

This excellent short hike derives its name from a Cherokee legend in which a young maiden threw herself off the cliffs overlooking the French Broad when she learned of her lover's death.

The yellow-blazed trail begins an easy-to-moderate ascent along a narrow, rocky trail among lots of poison ivy, Southern

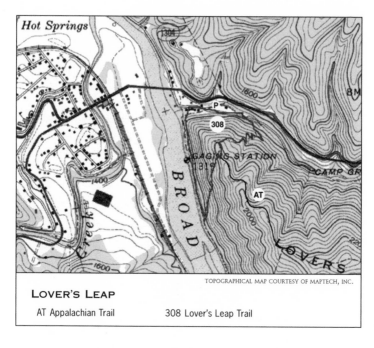

TOPOGRAPHICAL MAP COURTESY OF MAPTECH, INC.

LOVER'S LEAP

AT Appalachian Trail   308 Lover's Leap Trail

lady fern, galax, and Solomon's-seal. After 0.2 mile, you will reach a junction with the Pump Gap Trail (N 53' 26", W 48' 56"). Though not covered in this book, the Pump Gap Trail is an excellent day hike; a trail map and description are available at the Lover's Leap trailhead. Beneath you to the left is the Silvermine Campground. The Pump Gap Trail ascends to the left; the Lover's Leap Trail continues to the right. From here, you will begin a series of strenuous switchbacks through Eastern hemlock, chestnut oak, and striped maple. Almost 0.5 mile into the trail, you will reach an intersection with the Appalachian Trail (N 53' 27", W 49' 8"). The northbound Appalachian

Trail ascends sharply to the left; the southbound Appalachian Trail continues to the right. Immediately to the right is the first of the Lover's Leap overlooks, among lots of mountain laurel, fairy wand, white pine, and black birch. If you continue 20 yards to the left along the southbound Appalachian Trail, you'll come to a second, more impressive overlook (N 53' 24", W 49' 8"). The French Broad is ap-

Paint Rock near Hot Springs
PHOTO BY CAROLYN SAKOWSKI

proximately 500 feet below. Across the river and to the south (left) is Spring Creek Mountain. Directly across the river is Hot Springs, and behind Hot Springs stands Deer Park Mountain at 265° and 2 miles. In the far distance are the Paint Mountains in Tennessee. The Lover's Leap Trail descends along the Appalachian Trail for another 0.2 mile, where there is yet a third overlook (N 53' 20", W 49' 9"). As you descend to the river, you'll pass large clusters of mountain spiderwort and beardtongue. At 1 mile, the trail reaches the French Broad. It continues to the right alongside the river for 0.4 mile. The footpath ends at the

Nantahala Outdoor Center building at 1.3 miles (N 53' 30", W 49' 16"). From here, continue straight ahead until you reach the paved road. The parking lot is 0.25 mile to the right.

LAUREL RIVER TRAIL (#310)

Length: 3 or 4 miles, one way, depending on whether you turn left or right at Runion
Difficulty: easy
Elevation change: 200 feet
USGS quadrangle: Hot Springs
Access: If you are heading north on U.S. 25/U.S. 70, turn into the large gravel parking lot on the left (west) side of the road immediately before the junction with N.C. 208. There is a trail sign at the southern end of the parking area, near the creek (N 35° 54' 44", W 82° 45' 24").

This trail is an absolute must for wildflower enthusiasts. Unfortunately, the most common plant here is poison ivy, which is everywhere.

You will begin along a gravel path beneath lots of sycamore and locust; along the way are lots of sweet shrub, false Solomon's-seal, wood sorrel, yellow trillium, white violets, and sweet woodruff. The trail approaches a white house behind a dirt road at 0.2 mile, then veers to the right on a gravel road along private property (N 54' 33", W 45' 18"). A hundred yards past the house, you'll reach a large rock formation on the left side of the trail. This site is rich in wildflower diversity. A brief list of the plants found here includes jewelweed, Michaux's saxifrage, fire pink, true and false Solomon's-seal, Dutchman's-pipe, wild hydrangea, blackberry, white erect trillium, foamflower,

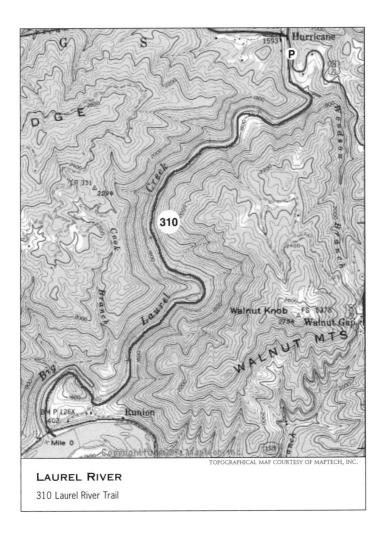

LAUREL RIVER

310 Laurel River Trail

toothwort, witch hazel, rue anemone, columbine, and yellow mandarin. A perfect picnic rock juts into the middle of the river at 0.6 mile (N 54' 27", W 35' 42"). A tenth of a mile later, the road forks. Take the right fork and continue along the river. The trail crosses a small spring at 1 mile. This marks the end of the private property and the beginning of the national forest; look for bishop's-cap and star chickweed nearby (N 54' 19", W 45' 47"). A few hundred yards later, the gorge narrows into some rapids. At 1.5 miles, you'll come to an 0.25-mile-long, continuous string of spectacular swimming holes lined with wild geraniums. The river forks at 2.4 miles, creating a small island dotted with *Elymus riparius*, an endangered wild rye grass (N 53' 40", W 45' 54"). You will reach another small stream crossing 0.25 mile later; look for pussy-toes, purple phacelia, bloodroot, and hairy alumroot. You will approach a series of concrete support structures and a trail intersection at 2.9 miles (N 53' 11", W 46' 31"). At the intersection, you can go about 0.1 mile to the left to visit the old site of Runion, or you can continue straight ahead for an additional 1 mile to the French Broad. If you continue straight ahead, you will follow the river as it makes a sharp bend to the right. After 0.3 mile, the trail moves inland from the river and follows an old stone wall for 0.25 mile. It crosses a railroad just shy of the 4-mile mark (N 53' 4", W 46' 46"). Cross the tracks and descend toward the French Broad, where the trail ends beneath a box elder looking south on to the river (N 53' 2", W 46' 46").

APPENDIX

LOOP TRAILS

Black Balsam Loop #1

Black Balsam Loop #2

Black Balsam Loop #3

Black Balsam Loop #4

Graveyard Fields Trail

Big East Fork Loop #1

Big East Fork Loop #2

Daniel Ridge Loop Trail plus
Farlow Gap Trail

Caney Bottom Loop

Cat Gap Loop Trail
(two options)

Coontree Loop

Avery Creek Loop #1

Avery Creek Loop #2

Avery Creek Loop #3

Avery Creek Loop #4

Pink Beds Loop Trail

Pilot Cove/Slate Rock Creek
Trail (two options)

Duggers Creek Loop Trail

West Rim Loop #1

West Rim Loop #2

East Rim Loop

Harper Creek Loop #1

Harper Creek Loop #2

Harper Creek Loop #3

Harper Creek Loop #4

Balsam Nature Trail

Mount Mitchell Loop

Roan Gardens Loop

Hickey Fork Loop

Max Patch Loop Trail

Cherry Creek Trail/Appalachian
Trail Loop

Lover's Leap Trail

HIKES FOR CHILDREN AND THE ELDERLY

These hikes are neither long nor strenuous. There are no cliffs to endanger kids or creek crossings to hinder old folks.

Flat Laurel Creek Trail
Ivestor Gap Trail
Black Balsam Loop #3
Black Balsam Loop #4
Graveyard Fields Trail
Daniel Ridge Loop Trail
Twin Falls Trail
Devil's Courthouse Trail
Courthouse Falls Trail
Pink Beds Loop Trail
Mount Pisgah Trail
Linville Falls Trail
Plunge Basin Overlook Trail
Duggers Creek Loop Trail

Pine Gap Trail
Bynum Bluff Trail
North Harper Creek Falls Trail
North Harper Creek Access Trail
Darkside Cliffs Trail
Mount Mitchell Summit Trail
Balsam Nature Trail
Mount Mitchell Loop Trail
Cloudland Trail
Roan Gardens Loop
Bald Knob Ridge Trail
Elk Falls Trail
Max Patch Loop Trail

HALF-DAY (OR LESS) HIKES

Sam Knob Summit Trail
Sam Knob Trail
Black Balsam Loop #1
Black Balsam Loop #2
Black Balsam Loop #4
Graveyard Fields Trail
Big East Fork Trail
Daniel Ridge Loop Trail
Caney Bottom Loop
Cat Gap Loop Trail
Coontree Loop
Avery Creek Loop #1
Devil's Courthouse Trail
Pink Beds Loop Trail
Mount Pisgah Trail
Pilot Cove Loop Trail
Linville Falls Trail
Plunge Basin Overlook Trail
Linville Gorge Trail (Blue Ridge
    Parkway)

Duggers Creek Loop Trail
West Rim Loop #1
Hawksbill Trail
Table Rock Summit Trail
North Harper Creek Falls Trail
North Harper Creek
    Access Trail
Big Lost Cove Cliffs Trail
Little Lost Cove Cliffs Trail
Darkside Cliffs Trail
Hickory Branch Trail
Mount Mitchell Summit Trail
Balsam Nature Trail
Mount Mitchell Loop Trail
Cloudland Trail
Roan Gardens Loop
Bald Knob Ridge Trail
Elk Falls Trail
Max Patch Loop Trail
Lover's Leap Trail

FULL-DAY HIKES

Art Loeb Trail III
Art Loeb Trail IV
Cold Mountain Trail
Black Balsam Loop #3
Black Balsam Loop #4
Big East Fork Loop #1
Big East Fork Loop #2
Art Loeb Trail II
Art Loeb Trail I
Daniel Ridge Loop Trail plus
    Farlow Gap Trail
Avery Creek Loop #2
Avery Creek Loop #3
Summey Cove Trail plus
    Courthouse Falls Trail

Slate Rock Creek Trail
Linville Gorge Trail
West Rim Loop #2
Shortoff Mountain Trail
East Rim Loop
Harper Creek Trail
North Harper Creek Trail
Harper Creek Loop #2
Harper Creek Loop #3
Harper Creek Loop #4
Woods Mountain Trail
Cherry Creek Trail/Appalachian
    Trail Loop
Laurel River Trail

TRAILS ACCESSIBLE FROM THE BLUE RIDGE PARKWAY

Sam Knob Summit Trail
Sam Knob Trail
Little Sam Knob Trail
Flat Laurel Creek Trail
Ivestor Gap Trail
Art Loeb Trail III
Graveyard Fields Trail
Art Loeb Trail II
Devil's Courthouse Trail
Mount Pisgah Trail
Linville Falls Trail
Plunge Basin Overlook Trail

Linville Gorge Trail (Blue Ridge Parkway)
Duggers Creek Loop Trail
Woods Mountain Trail
Mount Mitchell Summit Trail
Balsam Nature Trail
Camp Alice Trail
Commissary Trail
Old Mount Mitchell Trail
Mount Mitchell Loop Trail
Bald Knob Ridge Trail

INDEX